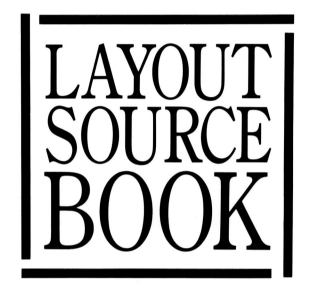

JULY 1950   TWO SHILLINGS & SIXPENCE NET

Art and Industry, Britain, 1950, by Zero.

LAYOUT SOURCE BOOK

ALAN SWANN

THE WELLFLEET PRESS

WELLFLEET

A Quarto Book

Published by Wellfleet Press
110 Enterprise Avenue
Secaucus, New Jersey 07094

ISBN 1-55521-530-0

This book was designed and produced by
Quarto Publishing plc
The Old Brewery, 6 Blundell Street
London N7 9BH

Senior Editor Susanna Clarke
Assistant Art Director Chloë Alexander

Editor Lydia Darbyshire

Designer Alan Swann

Picture Researchers Paul Diner, Sandra Bissoon

Art Director Moira Clinch
Editorial Director Carolyn King

Typeset by Ampersand Typesetting (Bournemouth) Ltd
Manufactured in Hong Kong by Regent Publishing Services Ltd
Printed by Leefung-Asco Printers Ltd, Hong Kong

CONTENTS

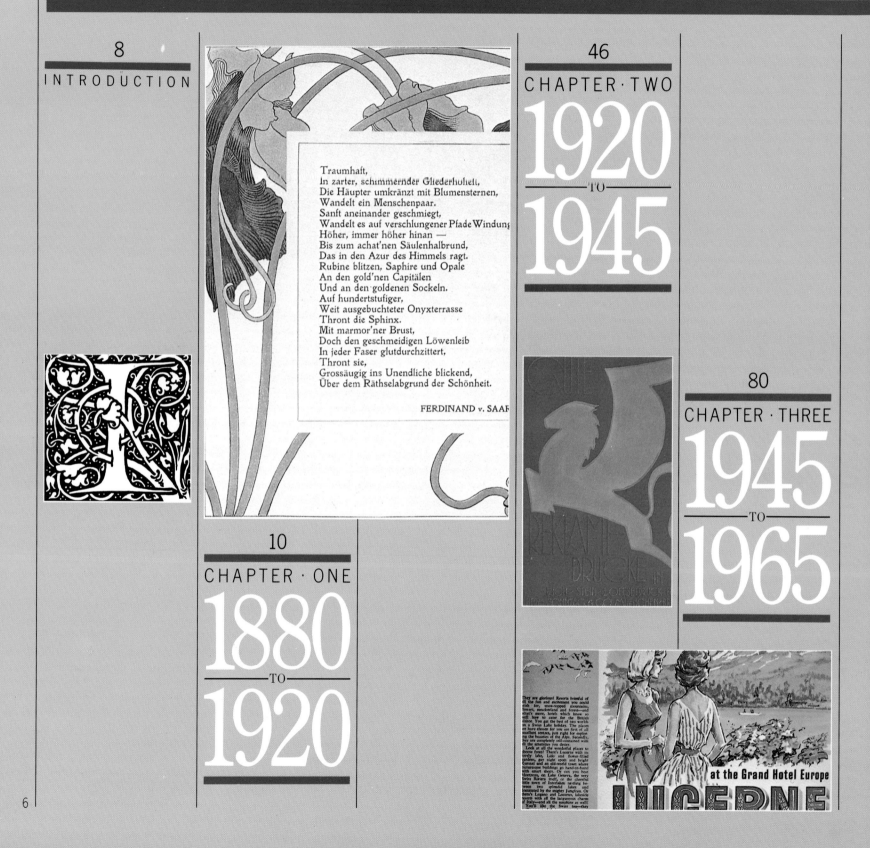

Traumhaft,
In zarter, schimmernder Gliederhoheit,
Die Häupter umkränzt mit Blumensternen,
Wandelt ein Menschenpaar.
Sanft aneinander geschmiegt,
Wandelt es auf verschlungener Pfade Windung
Höher, immer höher hinan —
Bis zum achat'nen Säulenhalbrund,
Das in den Azur des Himmels ragt.
Rubine blitzen, Saphire und Opale
An den gold'nen Capitälen
Und an den goldenen Sockeln.
Auf hundertstufiger,
Weit ausgebuchteter Onyxterrasse
Thront die Sphinx.
Mit marmor'ner Brust,
Doch den geschmeidigen Löwenleib
In jeder Faser glutdurchzittert,
Thront sie,
Grossäugig ins Unendliche blickend,
Über dem Räthselabgrund der Schönheit.

FERDINAND v. SAAR

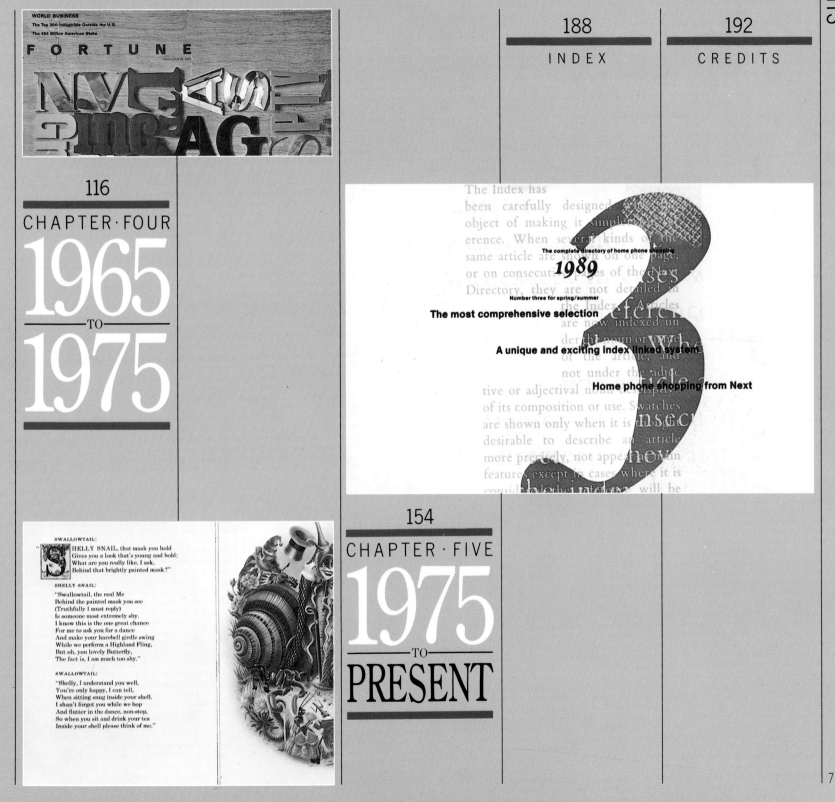

INTRODUCTION

Rarely does one have the opportunity to bring together in one book the work of selected designers and artists from a century which has seen so many changes.

It is easy with today's technology to take for granted some of the achievements that are presented in this book. However, in order to appreciate the creative quality of those achievements it is necessary to take account of the materials and technology available to the designer when the work was conceived. Although progress has made layout design more efficient over the years, it still takes a creative mind to manipulate the technology and materials into yielding exceptional work.

In seeking material for this book, choices had to be made concerning the best representations of layout design for each period of the past century. The first and the most important decision was to divide the book into historical periods that reflect social, technological and artistic developments as well as representing landmarks in the progress of the last hundred years. By using the two World Wars as pivotal events it has been possible to depict changing attitudes and to see the shift in thought that has given rise to a new breed of artist/designer.

Clearly there have been some major artistic events that have helped shape and advance the process of layout design. These have usually evolved from a society no longer willing to adhere to old standards and in search of a new identity on which to base its future. Although these movements have not been documented in detail here, they have undoubtedly exercised a key influence on their own periods and the time beyond.

Another factor of major importance must be the advances in technology which have either set about revolutionizing and inspiring layout design or, on the contrary, have been rejected as encroaching upon the pure artistic experience. At times these two opposing attitudes appear alongside each other, which adds interest to the period in question by demonstrating how two completely different viewpoints can result in two equally high-quality layouts.

It is worth remembering that every contributor to this book has been influenced by the time in which they lived, and by those artists or designers from all periods who inspired or encouraged their work. Each of the layouts shown on these pages contains elements that make it both interesting and unique. To gain the full effect and appreciate the work for its quality, it is important to view the layout in its entirety and also to note the subtleties and techniques implicit in the elements. Clearly, individual preference will play its part in determining each reader's response to a particular period or style, but we would do well to learn from all that is on offer, because no one period, style or point of view holds precedence over another.

In short, it is beneficial to absorb as many images as possible to shape the future of layout design, remembering that over the past century there have been some key pieces of work. *Mise en Page,* which is featured in this book, is one such example. In its time it presented the creative achievements of great art and contemporary technology and channelled them into a unique, exciting and forward-looking publication. Its influence was to inspire page layout and, more particularly, advertising layout for at least two decades after its appearance in 1931.

This book with its broad range of visual ideas, explores the vital thinking behind the images and sets out to inspire today's designers in their endeavours to communicate through good layout design.

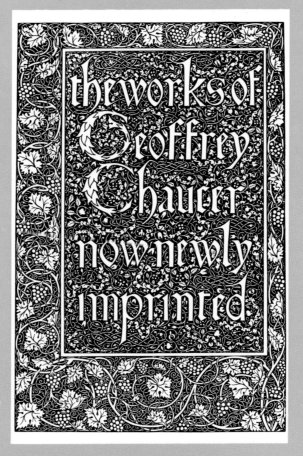

Woodcut title page by William Morris.

CHAPTER · ONE

1880 TO 1920

INTRODUCTION

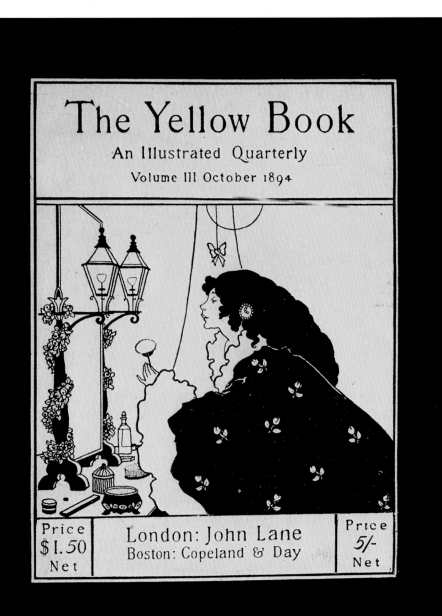

The Yellow Book, *Britain, 1894, published by John Lane. Aubrey Beardsley designed the first four issues of the magazine, the content of which was influential in the development of the arts at the time. Beardsley ceased to illustrate the publication in 1895 in the wake of the Oscar Wilde scandal.*

To understand what was happening to the design and layout of written information in the late 19th century, it is necessary to take three factors into account. First, the climate of the arts at this time, when exciting and innovative visual styles were being generated throughout Europe and America. Fine artists, such as Sir Edward Burne-Jones, were diversifying and experimenting with the means of communicating with a wider audience. Burne-Jones was closely associated with Rossetti and the Pre-Raphaelite Brotherhood, and he also influenced some of William Morris's designs and layouts. This synergy and interaction was reflected in artistic life throughout Europe.

The second factor was the huge advance in technology, especially the technology of print. Refined, machine-made papers and fast, accurate print production made it possible to offer relatively inexpensive reading matter to an increasing and appreciative audience.

The third factor was the energy that was being devoted to the development of mass-education and literacy. As countries became industrialized and more and more factories appeared, the need for wider and better education arose so that more of the workforce could carry out tasks that involved reading and writing. The increasing demand for educational tools was accompanied by a widespread growth in the literary and visual arts. The arts and what they had to offer became a part of everyday life, entertaining and educating an audience with a healthy appetite for the stimuli this visual material had to offer.

A New Breed of Artist

Artists' works no longer simply hung in galleries. The new commercial printing presses needed art, and commercial artists, the forerunners of graphic designers, were in the vanguard of change. The status enjoyed by these skilled craftsmen with their knowledge of the techniques involved in print production encouraged the growth of a new breed of artist. At the same time, the traditional loyalties of fine artists were undergoing major shifts, as opportunities arose for a new generation of creative talent, eager to try out different ways of making images while communicating with a larger and more attentive audience.

The New Magazines

John Lane, the proprietor of the Bodley Head, one of the leading publishers of the time, engaged the services of the talented and distinctive Aubrey Beardsley (1872-98) to decorate his fashionable list of popular authors. Lane's enthusiasm, fired by the artistic fervour of the international art set, led to the publication between 1894 and 1897 of the quarterly magazine *The Yellow Book*, which was published in both England and

America as a review of the activity and trends in the art world. Several of the covers were designed by Beardsley, and its contents, presented in a two-column format, were light, refreshing and readable.

In America, where the approach to design and the modern technology was more commercially oriented, type-founders encouraged and financed the development of new typefaces. The *Century Illustrated Monthly* magazine underwent a dramatic change in its appearance when Theodore Low de Vinne, its proprietor and a noted scholar of typography, commissioned a typeface for use in the publication. Linn Boyd Benton designed the New Century Typeface to give this magazine its distinctive and original appearance and so started a trend in the creation of design layouts that would be recognizable as a "house style".

In Europe a host of sophisticated arts magazines was available. Art Nouveau manifested itself in *Die Jugend* and *Ver Sacrum*, in which literature and trends in the fine arts were reviewed and encouraged.

Jugend ("Youth") was closely associated with the Art Nouveau movement Jugendstil, which took its name from the German publication. The finest artists available created a page styling that was both bold and distinctive. Perfectly justified columns of type in a light black typeface were punctuated with bolder letters of the same fount, while illustrations were used to bring pages to life. Carefully designed visual patterns emerge from each spread. The use of illustration and well-proportioned typographic layout made it a stylistic leader at this period.

The Viennese magazine *Ver Sacrum* ("Sacred Spring") displays perhaps more sensitivity than *Jugend*. A magnificent use of white space, with pages often incorporating illustrations by such leading European artists as Gustav Klimt, appealed to a highly sophisticated audience with a deep and serious interest in the arts.

In Germany, *Simplicissimus*, a satirical arts review, treated its public to a lively, large-format periodical with fine-quality illustrations that depicted the social dilemmas of the period. Carefully used, well-selected colour tints punctuate the lengthy reviews, which were commissioned from a host of talented contributors. These included Thomas Theodor Heine who created the famous bulldog mascot for the magazine; Rudolf Wilke, a master sketcher of the comic side of social mores; Heinrich Zille, better known as a book illustrator; Bruno Paul whose work brought an Art Nouveau style to the magazine; as well as many occasional contributors such as Käthe Kollwitz and Georg Grosz.

Jugend, *Germany, 1905. This magazine, whose name means "Youth", was the inspirational force behind Jugendstil.*

The New Audience and Book Design

The Germans found inspiration in a new, wealthy, materialistic audience, and they developed and exploited the new technology. German artists employed their skills and talents in creating new typefaces and in the development of commercial products. Large type-foundries flourished as the industry strove to keep up with the trends in typography, and influential publishing centres developed in Leipzig and Berlin. The publishing firm Insel Verlag was noted for the quality of its book design, and in 1905 the octavo-sized pocket book introduced a new approach to popular book design, pre-dating the Penguin concept in England and making handy, pocket-sized literature available to the masses.

Simplicissimus, *Germany, c. 1905. Originally conceived as a literary magazine by its publisher Albert Langen, its energetic and clever response to the corruption of the ruling classes made it the most influential voice for cartoonists and polemic writers. It was modelled on the Parisian satirical journal* Gil Blas *and employed the best graphic humorists of the time.*

INTRODUCTION

Newspapers

Changing attitudes in Europe manifested themselves in new ideas in newspaper promotion. The *Daily Mirror*, launched in 1903 by Lord Northcliffe to provide "gentlewomen" with their own publication, derived its title from the traditional image of the woman's pastime of looking in the mirror. Northcliffe's forward thinking was not admired by the traditional, "serious" newspapers, which thought that the *Daily Mirror* was a grotesque fiasco. Its bold headings, large pictures and fewer columns than the other dailies were seen as being of inferior quality to its wordy and austere competitors, among which *The Times* of London continued to be regarded as the visual benchmark. The eight-column format, broadsheet style that *The Times* preferred was crammed with small type, which resulted in a consistently grey column pattern with an occasional, hardly noticeable heading, never exceeding a single column width. Its front page carried only social and personal announcements, reflecting the social priorities of its readers. Its format, more or less unchanged for a century, retained its worthy image long after the picture newspapers had become everyday items. American newspapers, on the other hand, less constrained by tradition, were eager to exploit the new print production processes.

Modern printing presses made it possible to mass-produce high-quality reproductions of artists' illustrations in colour and even to manipulate photographs and type. Commercial businesses were quick to use this wonderful new art form, although only more prosperous concerns could invest in this process. Commercial artists were required both to understand methods of printing and to create highly realistic representations of life as seen through the public eye. Examples of this can be seen in the programme of Sir Henry Irving's 1916 production of *The Barton Mystery* at the Savoy theatre, where one colour was used to great effect. In Huntley & Palmer's 1903 catalogue, the availability of colour printing enabled the designer to produce a sensitive and accurate layout, whose quality could be controlled throughout a massive print-run.

Evening Standard, Britain, 1918. This page integrates serious comment on military affairs with lighthearted editorial comment on the fashion of the day. Display and classified advertisements are laid out on the four-column grid.

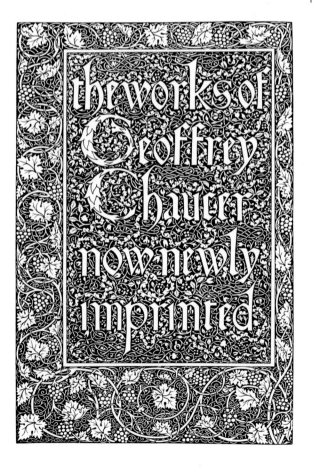

The works of Geoffrey Chaucer now newly imprinted, *Britain, 1896. Designed by William Morris for the Kelmscott Press. The title page and first page reveal the highly decorative woodcut designs. The type, illustration and design layout were inspired by Morris's interest in incunabula, and his intention was to free craftsmen from the laborious tasks of manual labour in the factories and to reinstate dignity in the so-called minor arts and crafts. He was inspired by John Ruskin and his formation of the Guild of St George in 1878 and by the ideals of the Pre-Raphaelite Brotherhood.*

The Private Presses

Artists like William Morris also flourished in this period, but for different reasons. Eschewing the new technology, Morris emphasized the importance of treating print and printed images as a pure art form and inspired other artists and publishers. The private presses that emerged in England and, later, in America were a direct response to his pioneering work. Even the young artist from France, Lucien Pissarro (1863-1944), found a home for his publishing ideas in England, where, supported by his father, Camille, he founded the Eragny Press. Pissarro's own skills and knowledge were enhanced by his association with artists and craftsmen such as Charles Ricketts (1866-1931). Like Morris, Pissarro was keen to be involved in the production of all the elements, from paper to type-founts, which were lovingly combined with exquisite illustrations and the occasional use of colour to produce memorable and beautifully laid out pages.

Each of the private presses had its own group of distinguished artists and craftsmen, with their individual and unique styles of working. This renaissance in layout design produced many figures who later became leaders in publishing and design. The work of Edward Johnston (1872-1944) for the Doves Press, for example, emphasized a different approach from that of Morris. His uncluttered calligraphic style exploited the page as a white space and not as an area to be completely adorned with decoration.

At the same time as these master artists and craftsmen were indulging in their grand ideals, the more commercial publishing houses were learning about the importance of visual presentation. The public, both in Europe and America, was eager to explore and enjoy the hitherto unknown worlds now revealed through the medium of print. Magazines sprang into existence to offer their own type of experience, and, for the wealthy, fashion and travel became an essential part of this new social awareness.

Europe became the centre of this awakening, and lively printed material was being produced everywhere. The privileged classes were enjoying the final years of an era in which the industrial wisdom of the West seemed to dominate the entire world. The outbreak of World War I suddenly and dramatically stopped this extravagance of creative energy. The shock of the war years caused a rethink in the styling and imagery of the past and led to the key changes in design that are now recognized as being the major force behind 20th-century layout design.

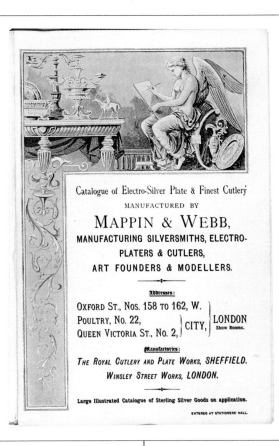

Mappin & Webb, Britain, 1890. This fashionable retailer and jeweller uses the elegant new style of illustration to frame the mixture of typeface styles, laid out to emphasize the company's classical traditions and the modern aspects of its products through the use of a sans serif typeface. It was produced by technically advanced methods.

The Century Illustrated Magazine, USA, 1886. Later issues of this magazine, printed by De Vinne in New York, led to the commissioning of Century Typeface, which was designed by Linn Boyd Benton.

Machines and Design

As machines became capable of producing a wider range of functional items in greater quantity, craftsmen and their skills became obsolete and less cost-effective. Craftsmen themselves realized that they could not compete with mass-production and began to look to the factories for employment and the better pay and conditions offered.

In 1909 the First Futurist Manifesto was written by the Italian Filippo Tommaso Marinetti (1876-1944) and was published in *Le Figaro* in France in the same year. Marinetti's passion for speed and violent upheaval, inherent in the manufacture of vast new machines, gave visual stimulation to a new form of imagery. The old, sentimental, bourgeois style, with its flowery decoration and taint of decadence, was to be toppled in favour of a new era of art and design.

Marinetti's ideas formed the basis for a new style of functional design that was applied especially by Russian artists to the visual and graphic communication ideas that were beginning to emerge before the massive changes that were to take place after the 1917 Revolution.

1. *Woodcut, Japan. The 19th century saw the importation of delicate Japanese art to Europe. The highly stylized linear designs of these pieces had a profound effect on Western art of this period, affecting the work of James Whistler, Aubrey Beardsley and, later, Pablo Picasso.*

2. *Door, Britain, c.1900. Designed by Charles Rennie Mackintosh (1868-1928) for the Willow Tea Rooms, Glasgow. Largely ignored by the English Arts & Crafts movement, Mackintosh and his group, The Four, had a great influence over the artists of the Viennese Sezession, and he exhibited in Vienna in 1900 and in Turin in 1902. His most obvious influence appears in Ver Sacrum, the magazine of the Sezession.*

3. *Tile, Britain, c.1890. The highly stylized peonies are typical of the use of nature as a source for design in the late 19th century.*

4. *Bible, Germany, c.1456. Early printing, with its hand-crafted quality, was a major inspiration for William Morris's Kelmscott Press and had a direct influence on the private presses.*

5

6 |

77

Narnach über ein kleine zeit
Kam her aus ferren launden weit
Ein kürriser gar hochberümbt
Desselben lob was weyt geplumbt
Wie Er het manchen kampff gethan
Darinn Im nyemandt het gesyget an
Desselben kempffers Erenhold
Rüefft aus wer mit im kempfen wolt   A iii

5. *William Holman Hunt (1827-1910), Britain, c.1850. A founder member, with Dante Gabriel Rossetti and Sir John Everett Millais, of the Pre-Raphaelite Brotherhood in 1848. Their influence was on all aspects of design, from the Gothic revival style of architecture to the illustrations used by the private presses.*

6. Tewrdannck, *Germany, 1517. The images created by medieval artists and the calligraphic style of manuscripts were a source of inspiration to typographers and designers.*

NEW TYPEFACES

1

A B C D E F G H I J
K L M N O P Q R S
T U V W X Y Z
1 2 3 4 5 6 7 8 9 0
a b c d e f g h i j k l m n o p q r s t u v w x y z

2

ABCDEFGHIJKLMNOPQRSTUV
WXYZ
abcdefghijklmnopqrsftuvwxyz
1234567890

3

ABCDEFGHIJKLMNOPQRSTUVWXYZ

abcdefghijklmnopqrstuvwxyz

1234567890

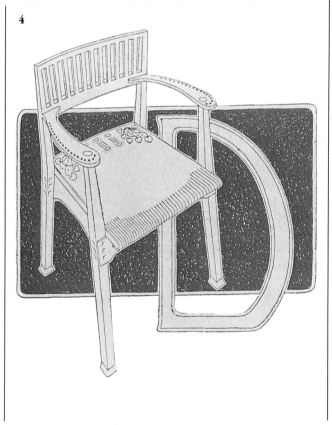

4

5

NEWS FROM NOWHERE OR
AN EPOCH OF REST.
CHAPTER I. DISCUSSION AND
BED.

P at the League, says a friend, there had been one night a brisk conversational discussion, as to what would happen on the Morrow of the Revolution, finally shading off into a vigorous statement by various friends, of their views on the future of the fully-developed new society.

AYS our friend: Considering the subject, the discussion was good-tempered; for those present, being used to public meetings & after-lecture debates, if they did not listen to each other's opinions, which could scarcely be expected of them, at all events did not always attempt to speak all together, as is the custom of people in ordinary polite society when conversing

6

ABCDEFGHIJKLM
NOPQRSTUV
WXYZ &

abcdefghijklmnopqrstuvwxyz
æœfifffflffifl 1234567890

7

ABCDEFGHIJKLMNOPQRSTUVWXYZ
abcdefghijklmnopqrstuvwxyz
1234567890

8

ABCDEFGHIJKLMNOPQRSTU
VWXYZ
abcdefghijklmnopqrstuvwxyz
1234567890

1. Capital letter, Britain, 1896. Designed by William Morris for the Works of Geoffrey Chaucer (top left). Golden type, designed by William Morris in 1890, was based on the Venetian typefaces produced by Nicolas Jenson in the 15th century.
2. Eckmann, Germany, 1900. Produced for the Klingspor founders, the face was influenced by the trend towards Art Nouveau.
3. Herold, Germany, 1901.
4. Ver Sacrum, *Austria, 1900.*
5. News From Nowhere, *Britain, 1892. This page, printed at the Kelmscott Press, shows a layout using Golden type.*
6. Troy type, Britain, 1892. Morris's second type was based on black type of 15th-century Germany.
7. Century, USA, 1895. Produced for The Century Illustrated Monthly Magazine *by Linn Boyd Benton.*
8. Franklin Gothic, USA, c.1903.

1. Jugend, *Germany, 1905. This magnificent publication from Munich, from which the German style of Art Nouveau derived the name Jugendstil, was most influential.*

3

1

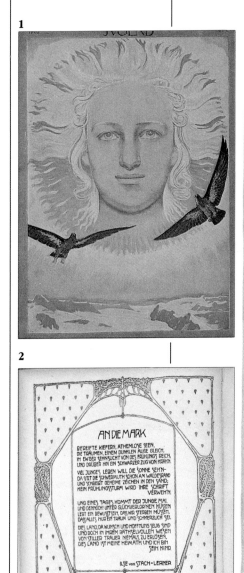

2

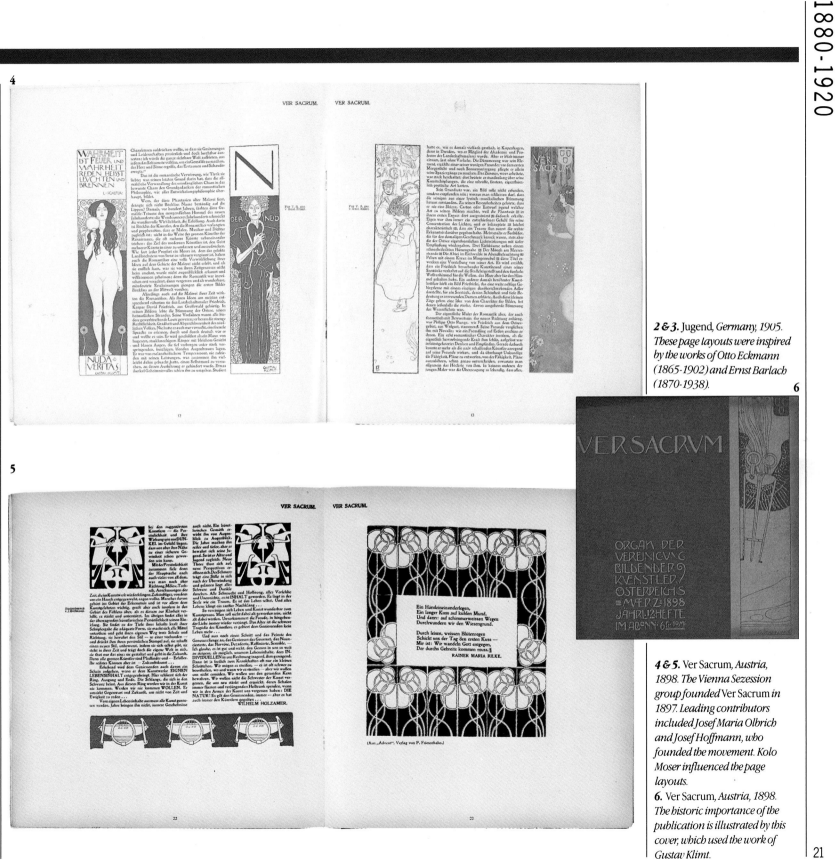

2 & 3. Jugend, *Germany, 1905. These page layouts were inspired by the works of Otto Eckmann (1865-1902) and Ernst Barlach (1870-1938).*

4 & 5. Ver Sacrum, *Austria, 1898. The Vienna Sezession group founded* Ver Sacrum *in 1897. Leading contributors included Josef Maria Olbrich and Josef Hoffmann, who founded the movement. Kolo Moser influenced the page layouts.*

6. Ver Sacrum, *Austria, 1898. The historic importance of the publication is illustrated by this cover, which used the work of Gustav Klimt.*

ARTS MAGAZINES

1. Simplicissimus, *Germany,* *c.1905. The lively, critical journal displayed the works of all the major contemporary artists and designers of its time.*

2. The Studio, *Britain, 1894. Launched in 1893 as the first Art Nouveau magazine, this layout includes the work of Aubrey Beardsley.*

3. The Idler, *Britain, 1894. A monthly arts magazine, edited by Jerome K. Jerome and Robert Barr, echoed the visual layout of its time, but incorporated Beardsley's distinctive illustration.*

4. Radiantismo, *Italy, 1917. This publication was Natalia Goncharova's and Mikhail Larionov's statement on the new form of art, Rayonism, which combined the notions of Cubism and Russian peasant art, and concerned itself with reflected rays of light from different objects. The layout is modern, even by today's standards.*

5. Gil Blas, *France, 1895. The fictional early 18th-century character Gil Blas lent his name to this satirical and rather naughty turn-of-the-century publication.*

6. Gil Blas, *France, 1895. This illustrated spread shows the somewhat daring illustrations.*

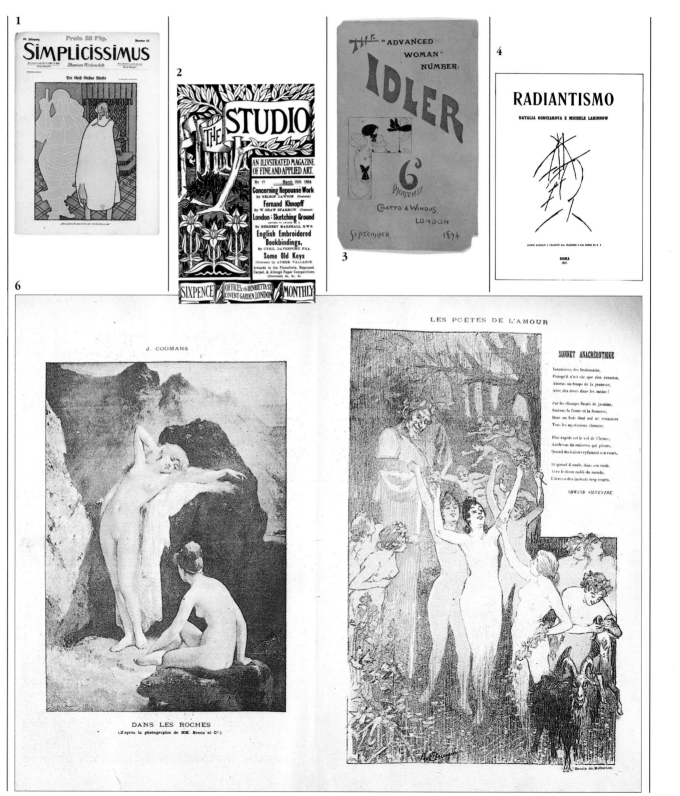

7. The Savoy, Britain, 1896.
This quarterly ran for only eight
issues. The editor was Arthur
Symons, and Aubrey Beardsley
was art editor. It was published
by Leonard Smithers at the
Chiswick Press of Charles
Whittingham & Co.
8 & 9. Simplicissimus, Germany,
1905-6. The wit and humour of
this lively publication are clearly
displayed in the top layout,
which includes illustrations by
Reznicek and Engl.

CONSUMER MAGAZINES

5.

1.

HARPER'S BAZAR

VOL. XXXVI
No. 7
JULY, 1902

THE STRENUOUS LIFE FOR GIRLS

BY HENRY VAN DYKE

Drawn by F. Y. CORY.
TRAGEDIES OF CHILDHOOD.
VII.—HIS FIRST PHOTOGRAPH.

7.

HARPER'S BAZAR
A·MONTHLY·MAGAZINE·FOR·WOMEN
JULY 1902
HARPER & BROTHERS

8.

THE ILLUSTRATED LONDON NEWS

9.

The Lady
SPRING DOUBLE NUMBER

10.

LIBERTY's SILK-VELVET
PUNCH
THE LIVERPOOL & LONDON & GLOBE INSURANCE CO. LTD.
FIRE LIFE ACCIDENT MARINE

6.

PUNCH, OR THE LONDON CHARIVARI.

BOYS OF THE DACHSHUND BREED.

6. Punch, *Britain, 1915. A typical spread, with bordered pages featuring satirical illustrations and text.*

7. Harper's Bazar, *USA, 1902. An interesting layout, with the magazine's masthead and styling dropped over the full colour illustration.*

8. The Illustrated London News, *Britain, 1918.*

9. The Lady, *Britain, 1896. An elegant, stylish magazine with a distinctive period feel.*

10. Punch, *Britain, 1915. This cover layout design by Richard Doyle (1824-83) was used from 1841 until 1956, the only exceptions being various special numbers.*

PRIVATE PRESSES

1

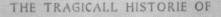

Ruse pour descouvrir les finesses de Amleth.

Ainsi furent deputez quelques courtisans, pour mener le Prince en quelque lieu escarté, dans le bois, et lesquels luy presentassent ceste femme, l'incitans à se souiller en ses baysers et embrassemens, artifices assez frequent de nostre temps, non pour essayer si les grands sont hors de leur sens, mais pour les priver de force, vertu et sagesse, par le moyen de ses sansues et infernales Lamies, produites par leurs serviteurs, ministres de corruption. Le pauvre Prince eust esté en danger de succomber à cest assaut, si un Gentil-homme, qui du vivant de Horvvendille, avoit esté nourry avec luy, ne se fust plus monstré ami de la nourriture prinse avec Amleth, que affec-

Corrupteurs de la jeunesse es courts des grands.

tionné à la puissance du tyran, lequel pourchassoit les moyens de envelopper le fils és pieges, esquels le pere avoit finy ses jours. Cestuy s'accompagna des courtisans deputez pour ceste trabison, plus avec deliberation d'instruire le Prince, de ce qu'il avoit à faire, que pour luy dresser des embusches et le trabir, estimant que le moindre indice qu'il donneroit de son bon sens, suffiroit pour luy faire perdre la vie. Cestuy-cy avec certains signes feit entendre à Amleth, en quel peril est ce qu'il se mettroit, si en sorte aucune il obeissoit aux mignardes caresses, et mignotises de la Damoyselle, envoyee par son oncle: ce qu'estonant le Prince esmeu de la beauté de la fille, fut par elle asseuré encor de la trabison: car elle l'aymoit de son enfance, et eust esté bien marie de son desastre et fortune, et plus de sortir de ses mains, sans jouyr de celuy qu'elle aymoit plus que soymesme. Ayant le jeune seigneur trompé les courtisans, et la fille, soustenans qu'il ne s'estoit avancé en sorte aucune à la violer, quoy qu'il dict du contraire, chacun s'asseura que veritablement il estoit insensé, et que son cerveau n'avoit force quelconque, capable d'apprehension raisonnable.

80

Enter Hamlet, and three of the Players.

Ham. Speake the speech I pray pou as I pronounc'd it to pou, trippingly on the tongue, but if pou mouth it as many of our Players do, I had as live the towne cryer spoke my lines, nor doe not saw the ayre too much with pour hand thus, but use all gently, for in the very torrent tempest, and as I may say, whirlwind of pour passion, pou must acquire and beget a temperance, that may give it smoothnesse, O it offends mee to the soule, to heare a robustious perwigpated fellowe tere a passion to totters, to very rags, to spleet the eares of the groundlings,

Plap. I warrant pour honour.
Ham. Be not too tame neither, but let pour owne discretion be pour tutor, sute the action to the word, the word to the action, with this speciall observance, that pou ore-steppe not the modestie of nature: For any thing so ore-doone, is from the purpose of playing, whose end both at the first, and nowe, was and is, to holde as twere

who for the most part are capable of nothing but inexplicable dumbe showes, and noyse: I would have such a fellow whipt for ore-dooing Termagant, it out-Herods Herod, pray pou avoyde it.

subtilty, such as one day might be prejudiciall to their prince, saying that under colour of such rudenes be shadowed a crafty pollicy, and by his devised simplicitye, be concealed a sharp and pregnant spirit, for which cause they counselled the king to try & know if it were possible, how to discover the intent and meaning of the yong prince, & they could find no better, nor more fit invention to intrap him then to set some faire, and beawtifull woman in a secret place, that with flattering speeches and all the craftiest meanes she could use, should purposely seeke to allure his mind to have his pleasure of her. for the nature of all young men, (specially such as are

Nature corrupted in man.

brought up wantonlie) is so transported with the desires of the flesh, and entreth so greedily into the pleasures thereof, that it is almost impossible to cover that foul affection neither yet to dissemble or hyde the same by art or industry, much less to shunne it. What cunning or subtilty so ever they use to cloak theire pretence, seeing occasion offered, and that in secret, specially in the most inticing sinne that rayneth in man, they cannot chuse (being constrayned by voluptuousnesse) but fall to naturall effect and working. To this end certaine courtiers were appointed to leade Hamblet into a solitary place within the woods, whether they brought the woman, inciting him to take their pleasures together, and to imbrace one another, but the subtill practises used in these our dayes, not to try if men of great account bee extract out of their wits, but rather to deprive them of strength, vertue, and wisedome, by meanes of such divelish practitioners, and infernall spirits their domestical servants, and ministers of corruption: and surely the poore prince at this assault had bin in great danger, if a gentleman (that in Horvendiles time had bin nourished with him) had not showne himselfe more

Subtilties used to discover Hamblets madnes.

81

1. Hamlet, *Germany, c.1890. Printed at Cranach in Weimar, with woodcuts by Edward Gordon Craig, this beautiful layout echoes the manuscripts of a past Gothic age.*

MAUD. BY ALFRED TENNYSON.

I HATE THE DREADFUL HOLLOW BEHIND THE LITTLE WOOD, ITS LIPS IN THE FIELD ABOVE ARE DABBLED WITH BLOOD-RED HEATH,
THE RED-RIBB'D LEDGES DRIP WITH A SILENT HORROR OF BLOOD,
AND ECHO THERE, WHATEVER IS ASK'D HER, ANSWERS DEATH.

2.

FOR THERE IN THE GHASTLY PIT LONG SINCE A BODY WAS FOUND,
HIS WHO HAD GIVEN ME LIFE: O FATHER! O GOD! WAS IT WELL?
MANGLED, & FLATTEN'D, AND CRUSH'D, AND DINTED INTO THE GROUND:
THERE YET LIES THE ROCK THAT FELL WITH HIM WHEN HE FELL.

2. *Design for Maud, Britain, 1893. Hand rendered as a layout guide for the engraver and printer, William Morris used pen, ink and watercolour.*
3 & 4. *Illuminated capitals, Britain, 1892. Incised from wood, these engraved, illuminated capitals were the hallmark of William Morris's unique and influential styling.*

3
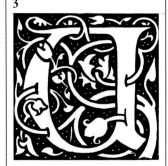

4

PRIVATE PRESSES

The Day of the Lord
Charles Kingsley

THE Day of the Lord is at hand, at hand!
  Its storms roll up the sky;
The nations sleep starving on heaps of gold;
  All dreamers toss and sigh;
The night is darkest before the morn,
When the clouds are heavy then breaks the dawn;
  And the Day of the Lord is at hand!
  The Day of the Lord is at hand!

Gather you, gather you, angels of God—
  Freedom and mercy and truth!
Oh, Come! for the earth is grown coward and old!
  Come down, and renew us her youth.
Wisdom, Self-Sacrifice, Daring and Love,
Haste to the battlefield, stoop from above,
  To the Day of the Lord at hand!
  The Day of the Lord at hand!

Gather you, gather you, hounds of Hell—
  Famine and Plague and War;
Idleness, Bigotry, Cant and Misrule,
  Gather, and fall in the snare!
Hireling, Mammonite, Bigot and Knave,
Crawl to the battlefield, sneak to your grave,
  In the Day of the Lord at hand!
  The Day of the Lord at hand!

154

IN THE BEGINNING

GOD CREATED THE HEAVEN AND THE EARTH. (AND THE EARTH WAS WITHOUT FORM, AND VOID; AND DARKNESS WAS UPON THE FACE OF THE DEEP, & THE SPIRIT OF GOD MOVED UPON THE FACE OF THE WATERS. (And God said, Let there be light: & there was light. And God saw the light, that it was good: & God divided the light from the darkness. And God called the light Day, and the darkness he called Night. And the evening and the morning were the first day. (And God said, Let there be a firmament in the midst of the waters, & let it divide the waters from the waters. And God made the firmament, and divided the waters which were under the firmament from the waters which were above the firmament: & it was so. And God called the firmament Heaven. And the evening & the morning were the second day. (And God said, Let the waters under the heaven be gathered together unto one place, and let the dry land appear: and it was so. And God called the dry land Earth; and the gathering together of the waters called he Seas: and God saw that it was good. And God said, Let the earth bring forth grass, the herb yielding seed, and the fruit tree yielding fruit after his kind, whose seed is in itself, upon the earth: & it was so. And the earth brought forth grass, & herb yielding seed after his kind, & the tree yielding fruit, whose seed was in itself, after his kind: and God saw that it was good. And the evening & the morning were the third day. (And God said, Let there be lights in the firmament of the heaven to divide the day from the night: and let them be for signs, and for seasons, and for days, & years: and let them be for lights in the firmament of the heaven to give light upon the earth: & it was so. And God made two great lights; the greater light to rule the day, and the lesser light to rule the night: he made the stars also. And God set them in the firmament of the heaven to give light upon the earth, and to rule over the day and over the night, & to divide the light from the darkness: and God saw that it was good. And the evening and the morning were the fourth day. (And God said, Let the waters bring forth abundantly the moving creature that hath life, and fowl that may fly above the earth in the open firmament of heaven. And God created great whales, & every living creature that moveth, which the waters brought forth abundantly, after their kind, & every winged fowl after his kind: & God saw that it was good. And God blessed them, saying, Be fruitful, & multiply, and fill the waters in the seas, and let fowl multiply in the earth. And the evening & the morning were the fifth day. (And God said, Let the earth bring forth the living creature after his kind, cattle, and creeping thing, and beast of the earth after his kind: and it was so. And God made the beast of the earth after his kind, and cattle after their kind, and every thing that creepeth upon the

27

1. A Roycroft Anthology, USA, c.1905. One of the important imitators of the English private presses was the Roycroft Press, under Elbert Hubbard, otherwise known as Fra. Elbertus, a strangely erudite man who appeared more concerned with image than content.

2. The Bible, Britain, 1903-5. Published by Doves Press with type designed by Edward Johnston, this page is a fine example of Johnston's page styling, with the unusual use of a capital letter fully extended to the length of the text.

Printer's Note

❧✦❧

THE conversation from Dibdin's Bibliographical Decameron, which I have here reprinted, was chosen partly for its own pleasant quality and partly because of its appropriateness to the purpose of this pamphlet. Later bibliographical research has no doubt superseded Dibdin's in accuracy and completeness, but to many of us the charm of his style is as engaging as ever and his taste in printing as unimpeachable; and this brief account of seven early Venetian printers, with its islands of text and oceans of commentary, supplies just the right material for displaying Mr. Goudy's Italian Old Style under various requirements of composition. The new type itself, though showing the study of several of the best early Italian faces, reminds me most strongly and admirably of Ratdolt's fine Roman. Single letters of the font are quite full and round enough to look well in lines of almost any length, and its close fitting makes it especially suitable for composition in narrow measures, as (I hope) the following pages will show. It was, too, an interesting problem to work out a title-page and initials reminiscent of the simple wood-cut designs of the great Venetians, and I found abundant material for them amongst the ornaments furnished by the Monotype Company, even though a few astronomical signs have been pressed into service. In the text initials only have I departed from conventional practice by making photo-engravings in reverse after the designs were composed, to give the black ground effect of the early Italian wood-cut initials.

The mention of islands, above, suggests to me that when my own time comes to be marooned on a desert island (by a party of no longer indulgent friends, whose books I haven't completed, or whose letters I haven't answered) instead of taking along the favorite volumes that most amateur castaways vote for, I think I shall arrange to be shipwrecked in company with a Monotype caster and a select assortment of ornamental matrices. The fascination and amusement—and the occasional happy result—that can be got out of the almost numberless combinations of a few simple units would enable me to cast away for an indefinite period with great contentment.

BRUCE ROGERS

❦

3. *Bruce Rogers, USA, c. 1920. This personal statement by Bruce Rogers shows his delight in setting type on the page. Rogers was a leading American practitioner of layout and design during the first part of the 20th century.*

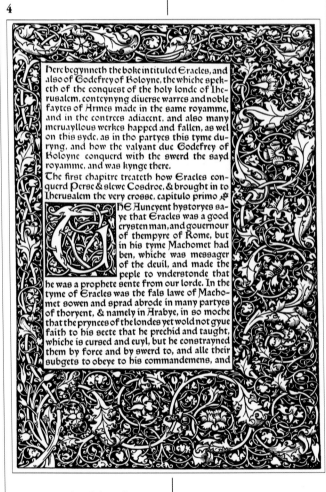

4. History of Godefrey of Boloyne, *Britain, 1893. Produced at the Kelmscott Press. The influence of Morris's decorative work paved the way for other designers both in England and in the United States.*

BOOKS

AFTER their first meeting, when Chopin played at a musicale, George Sand was apt to be there, too—they often came together. She was five years older than he, and looked fifteen, for his slight figure and delicate, boyish face gave him the appearance of youth unto the very last. In her letters to Madam Mariani, George Sand often refers to Chopin as "My Little One," and when some one spoke of him as "The Chopinetto," the name seemed to stick.

FREDERICK CHOPIN

That she was the man in the partnership is very evident. He really needed some one to look after him, provide mustard plasters and run for the camphor and the hot water bottle. He was the one who did the weeping and pouting, had the "nerves" and made the scenes; while she, on such occasions, would viciously roll a cigarette, swear under her breath, console and pooh-pooh.

Liszt has told us how on one occasion she had gone out at night for a storm-walk and Chopin, being too ill, or disinclined to go, remained at home. Upon her return she found him in a conniption, he having composed a prelude to ward off an attack of cold feet, and was now ready to scream through fear that something had happened to her. As she entered the door he arose, staggered and fell before her in a fainting fit ❧

77

1 & 2. Little Journeys, *Great Musicians Book 1,* USA, c. 1900. *Printed by the Roycroft Press. Despite Hubbard's overbearing methods of hand-producing books and the rather commercial approach, the quality and value of much of his work is unquestionable.*

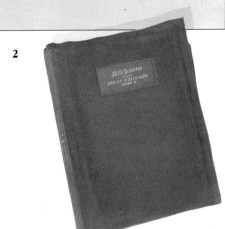

❀Ruth gleaneth in Boaz' field.

Go not to glean in another field, neither go from hence, but abide here fast by my maidens: ❀IX Let thine eyes be on the field that they do reap, & go thou after them: have I not charged the x   young

young men that they shall not **The** touch thee? and when thou art a‑ **Book of** thirst, go unto the vessels, & drink **Ruth.** of that which the young men have drawn.

❧X Then she fell on her face, and bowed herself to the ground, and said unto him, Why have I found grace in thine eyes, that thou shouldest take knowledge of me, seeing I am a stranger?

❧XI And Boaz answered & said unto her, It hath fully been shew‑ ed me, all that thou hast done un‑ to thy mother in law since the death of thine husband: and how thou hast left thy father and thy mother, & the land of thy nativity, & art come unto a people which thou knewest not heretofore,

❧XII The LORD recompense thy work, & a full reward be given thee of the LORD GOD of Israel, xi   under

3 & 4. The Book of Ruth and the Book of Esther, *Britain, 1896. Published by the Eragny Press. The woodcut was by Lucien Pissarro (1863-1944), son of the French Impressionist. Pissarro's self-imposed exile from France, because of the lack of interest in hand-made books there, brought him to England, where his association with figures such as Charles Ricketts inspired him to create completely hand-produced books.*

4

ILLUSTRATED BOOKS

1

GREY ROSES

BY HENRY HARLAND

LONDON: JOHN LANE, VIGO ST

BOSTON: ROBERTS BROS., 1895

2

The
Mirror of Music

BY STANLEY V. MAKOWER

LONDON: JOHN LANE, VIGO ST.

BOSTON: ROBERTS BROS., 1895

3

Yellow and White

BY

W. Carlton Dawe

London: John Lane, Vigo St.
Boston: Roberts Bros., 1895

4

AT THE
RELTON ARMS

BY EVELYN SHARP

LONDON: JOHN LANE, VIGO ST.

BOSTON: ROBERTS BROS., 1895

The
Bodley
Head

1, 2, 3 & 4. Title pages, Britain, 1894-5. Line block and letterpress, designed by Aubrey Beardsley for John Lane. Commercial book publishers looked for quality in layout and design for their popular titles. The Bodley Head, the forerunner of Penguin, is noted for its innovative and progressive development.

5. April Baby's Book of Tunes, Britain, c.1890. "Jack and Jill" by Kate Greenaway (1846-1901). By the 1890s the traditional coloured wood engravings, often produced by Edmund Evans, were becoming unfashionable and were making way for a new look in book illustration.

5

6

De la grâce externe & légère
Et qui me laiſſait plutôt coi
Font de vous un morceau de roi,
O conſtitutionnel, chère!

Toujours eſt-il, regret ou non,
Que je ne ſais pourquoi mon âme
Par ces froids penſe à vous, Madame
De qui je ne ſais plus le nom.

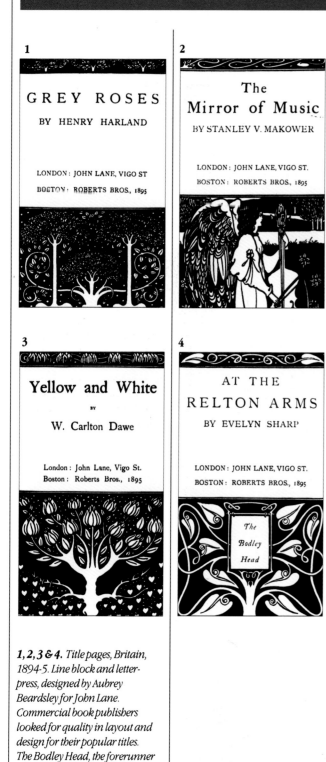

7

PUSS IN BOOTS.

A MILLER lay dying,—he made his last will;
He left his three sons his cat, ass, and mill:
To the eldest the mill, to the second the ass;
The third had the cat, and he cried out, "Alas!
I must starve now, unless I take Pussy to eat!"

6. Parallèlement, *France, 1900.
By Paul Verlaine (1844-96),
lithographs by Pierre Bonnard
(1867-1947), printed by Auguste
Clot, wood engravings by Tony
Beltrand, text printed by
L'Imprimerie Nationale. A
fashion for ethereal books
produced on unsewn Japanese
paper, with the notion that the
purchaser selects the binding of
his choice, started the trend
towards coffee-table books.*

7. Puss in Boots, *Britain,
c. 1900. Illustrated by Walter
Crane (1845-1915). Crane's
innovative styles allowed him
great freedom in choosing the
kind of work he undertook. This
page is a clear expression of a
new visual trend, incorporating
as it does type and illustration in
a way that was pioneered by the
Kelmscott Press in its early days.*

ILLUSTRATION & TEXT

1. Simplicissimus, *Germany,*
c.1909. Reznicek's illustrations
were often featured as they
complemented the publication's
progressive and adventurous
styling of layout.
4. Simplicissimus, *Germany,*
c.1909. A beautiful balance
between the page design and the
illustration by Reznicek shows
the designer's concern to use
space sympathetically and
sensitively.

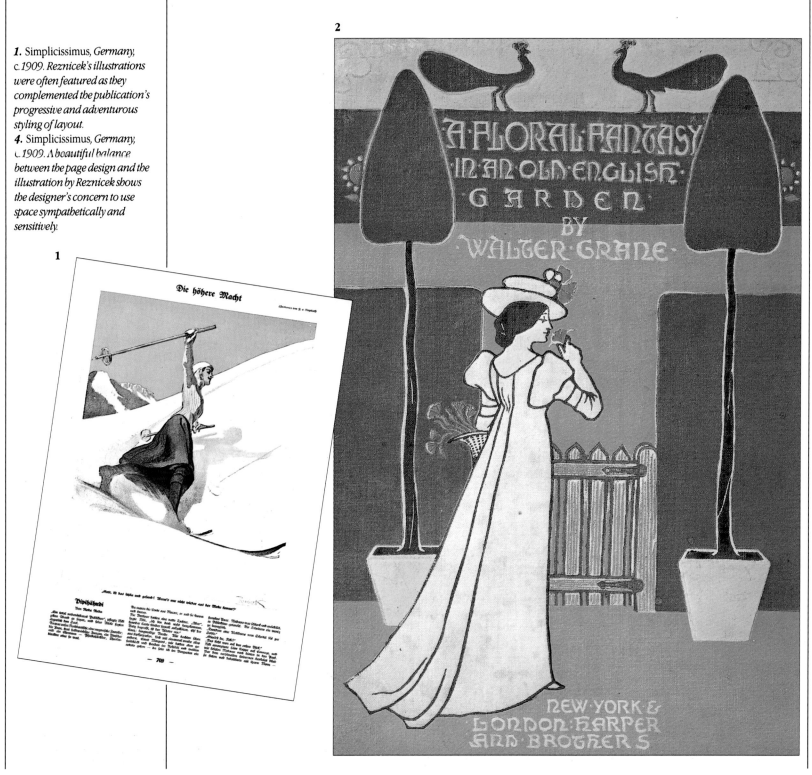

2. A Floral Fantasy in an Old English Garden, *Britain, c.1900. Illustrators such as Walter Crane would often create their own type images to balance the layout of the illustration and to retain an overall style.*
3. The Railroad Alphabet, *Britain, c.1902. Walter Crane's versatility and his competence in design are shown in this layout, which incorporates a completely different approach to type, illustration and layout.*

35

NEWSPAPERS

1 & 2. Daily Mirror, *Britain, 1912. Established in 1903 by Lord Northcliffe as an illustrated paper for women, it developed into a respected newspaper that covered major news stories. It adopted an inventive and innovative style of layout.*
3 & 4. The Times, *Britain, 1921. Established in the 18th century, the formal style was changed only rarely, with the occasional carefully placed illustration.*

7

5. Evening Standard, *Britain, 1918. An evening newspaper, the Standard expressed its news in a snappy, positive manner, with punchy headlines appearing across the full width of the page.*
6. Königsberger Harlungsche Zeitung, *Germany, 1914. News of the impending war is laid out in black type and formal columns in the characteristic German fashion.*
7. New York Times, *USA, 1916. Election news is laid out in a formal and distinguished manner. The special announcement is noted in a sans serif face, which stands out from the usual style.*

CATALOGS

1. *Liberty & Co., Britain, 1898.
Colonial furniture is sold from
the page, the numbered descriptions linked to the numbered
photographs alongside.*

2. *Liberty & Co., Britain, 1908.
The space surrounding the
individual items emphasizes the
qualities of the items in an
uncluttered way.*

3. *Furniture Gazette, Britain,
1889-90. This publication
displays new and fashionable
acquisitions from far afield. Its
use of various typefaces and
crisp, clear illustration
produced as line drawings,
describes with precision the items
available to wealthy Victorians.*

1

Bamboo Furniture (Anglo-Indian). Well made, strong and durable.

*Particulars and Prices
of the Examples illustrated:*

No. 1. **A Lady's Chair.** Made in bamboo. Seat and back upholstered with real Djijim-Kelims, in coloured designs.
Price 32/6.

No. 2. **A Bamboo Lamp** (or Flower-Pot) Stand.
Price 12/6.

No. 3. **A Venetian Hammered - Copper Vase.** Extremely elegant form.
Price 30/-.

No. 4. **An Artistic and Handsome Settee.** Made in selected and strong bamboo. Seat and back covered with real Djijim-Kelims, in coloured designs.
Price 57/6.

No. 5. **A Hand-carved Wooden Tray and Folding-Stand.** An excellent and artistic Four o'Clock Tea Table.
Price 50/- complete.

No. 6. **A Gentleman's Chair.** Made in bamboo. Seat and back handsomely upholstered in Djijim-Kelims (to match with No. 1).
Price 40/-.

No. 7. **A Draught-Screen.** Richly embroidered satin panels, mounted on carved wooden frame. Suitable for either Dining Room or Drawing Room.
Price 5 Guineas.

2

ENGLISH POTTERY, MADE FOR, AND OBTAINABLE ONLY FROM, LIBERTY & Co., OR THEIR AGENTS.
Original examples introduced by Liberty & Co. in practical shapes, made and decorated by hand. The surface of this beautiful pottery is enriched with lustrous and scintillating glazes.

No. 1. 8 ins. diameter. 13/6
No. 2. 4 ins. high. 10/6
No. 3. 8 ins. diameter. 9/3
No. 4. 6 ins. high. 6/9
No. 5. 6 ins. high. 5/-
No. 6. 9 ins. diameter. 10/6
No. 7. 9½ ins. high. 15/6
No. 8. 6 ins. diameter. 7/6, 9/6
No. 9. 9 ins. high. 17/6
No. 1. 7½ ins. high. 17/6

3

THE FURNITURE GAZETTE.

[FEB. 1, 1889.]
57

Out and About.

I.—NEEDHAM'S PATENT "FERRUMJUNGO" BAMBOO FURNITURE.

INFINITELY varied are the uses to which the bamboo is put by Eastern nations, and it is no exaggeration to say that most of the devices and appliances copied from European nations could be better spared by the natives than could this useful plant, which from its very origin to

FIG 1. FIG 2.

[natural] decay never ceases to produce something beneficial. [In] our own country, too, we have realised the usefulness of [the ba]mboo, though its applications are of a more limited [charac]ter, being mainly confined to the making of furniture [of an] ornamental and decorative character. This branch

[of ind]ustry has attained to a remarkable state of develop-[ment] in recent times, and among those who have con-[tribut]ed in advancing the manufacture is Mr. W. F. [NEED]HAM, of 69, Camden-street, Birmingham. His [factor]y consists of a large building three storeys high, and

here is brought into requisition every appliance adapted to expedite production, and to insure good workmanship. The several floors are connected with a lift, and every other needful provision is made to facilitate the carrying on of a large business. Stocks of raw materials, such as bamboo, canes, and timber, are kept on hand in consider-

able quantities, so that the works are equal to even the heaviest requirements.

The various classes of bamboo furniture here manu-factured are noteworthy alike for their lightness and

elegance, as well as for their substantial workmanship; and despite increased competition, Mr. Needham has for several years past made it his object to produce only work

which should have both novelty in design and strength of wear to recommend it. Not content with past achieve-ments he has lately completed and patented a new method

of construction, which we believe will insure for bamboo furniture a still greater amount of public favour than it has enjoyed in the past. Two methods have hitherto been adopted by different makers. Those making inferior goods have merely nailed the bamboo together, an altogether

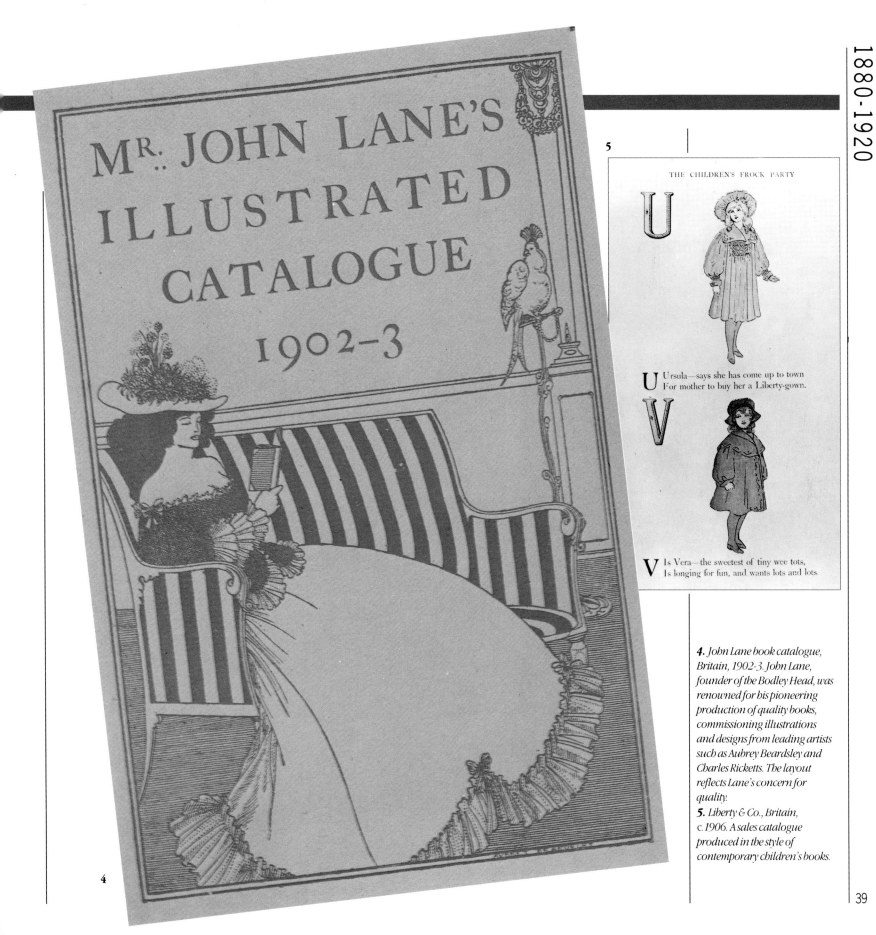

MR. JOHN LANE'S ILLUSTRATED CATALOGUE 1902-3

THE CHILDREN'S FROCK PARTY

U

U Ursula—says she has come up to town
For mother to buy her a Liberty-gown.

V

V Is Vera—the sweetest of tiny wee tots,
Is longing for fun, and wants lots and lots.

4. *John Lane book catalogue, Britain, 1902-3. John Lane, founder of the Bodley Head, was renowned for his pioneering production of quality books, commissioning illustrations and designs from leading artists such as Aubrey Beardsley and Charles Ricketts. The layout reflects Lane's concern for quality.*
5. *Liberty & Co., Britain, c.1906. A sales catalogue produced in the style of contemporary children's books.*

CATALOGS

1. *Silber and Fleming, Britain, 1889-90. This cunning engineering of the page, based originally on a five-column grid, is cleverly distorted by the geometrical positioning of the carefully proportioned scraperboard illustrations. The typeface and the positioning of trademarks give a dignified quality to the page.*

2. *Children's book listing, Britain, 1894. The mix of typefaces on this listing reflects the Victorian printers' method of communicating different aspects of the layout. The illustration occupies a disproportionate area of the layout, yet balances the overall effect.*

HUNTLEY & PALMERS'
CHRISTMAS CAKES

HOLLY.

NANSEN.

ICED SANDRINGHAM

MEXICAN.

ACADEMY.

CANTERBURY.

CHATSWORTH.

NOVELTY.

BANQUET.

ICED FRUIT.

ORNAMENTED SANDRINGHAM.

ICED ALMOND.

CHRISTMAS.

EMPRESS.

READING 1903 & LONDON

3. *Huntley & Palmer, Britain, 1903. This extremely decorative layout cleverly displays the products, while suggesting both quality and grandeur. The border emphasizes the festivity of the season, and the display type has been hand-rendered, as was common for this period. The product names have been centred beneath the illustrations.*

MENUS & THEATER PROGRAMS

1 & 2. The Barton Mystery, Britain, 1916. This programme from the Savoy Theatre is printed in an exquisite blue and features a photograph of Henry Irving, son of the famous actor and entrepreneur.

3 & 4. Moulin Rouge, France, c.1920. The contrast of style between the flamboyance of France and the restraint of the London Savoy programme, reflects the distinct difference of lifestyles of these two great cities.

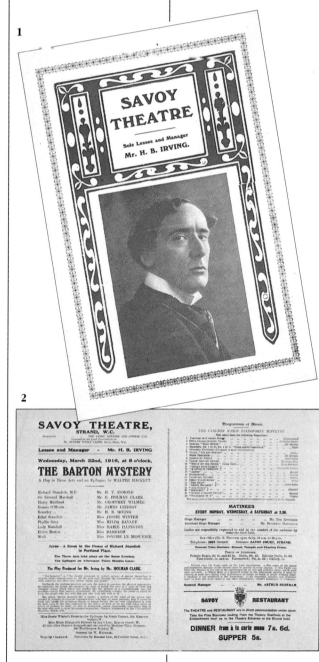

5

MENU

6

Complimentary Dinner
TO
Mᴿ GEORGE FLETT,
AT THE SAVOY HOTEL.
FEB.20ᵀᴴ 1908.

CANADA
NEW ZEALAND
AUSTRALIA
NATAL
CAPE COLONY
TRANSVAAL
ARGENTINE
BRAZIL
MEXICO
1883
1908
INDIA
STRAITS SETTLEMENT
HONG KONG
CHINA
BURMAH
SIAM
JAPAN
EGYPT
SPAIN

6 & 7. *Menu, Britain, 1908. Produced for a special dinner at the Savoy for Mr George Flett, the stunning array of visual information on the front is combined with a cunningly contrived layout incorporating a symbolic illustration.*

5. *Menu card, France, c.1920. This exquisitely cut-out menu card, featuring an ebullient waiter, is a lively and contemporary-looking piece of graphics that would be as successful today as it was when first produced.*

7

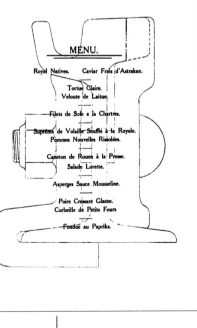

MENU.

Royal Natives.   Caviar Frais d'Astrakan.
Tortue Claire.
Veloute de Laitue.
Filets de Sole a la Chartres.
Suprême de Volaille Soufflé à la Royale.
Pommes Nouvelles Rissolées.
Caneton de Rouen à la Presse.
Salade Lorette.
Asperges Sauce Mousseline.
Poire Cressane Glacee.
Corbeille de Petits Fours
Fondue au Paprika.

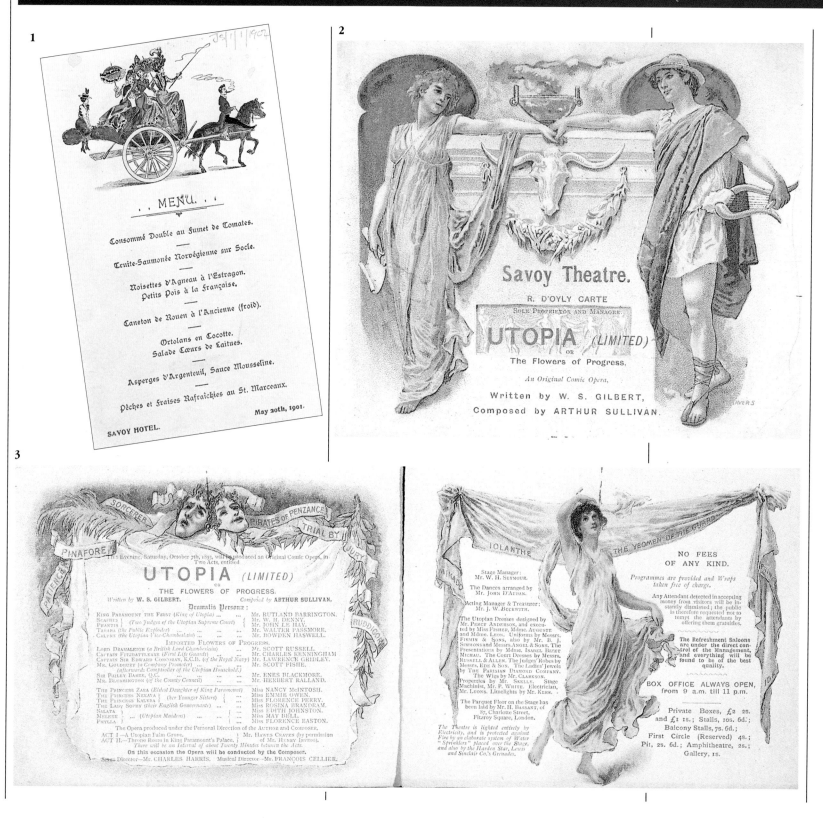

1

MENU.

Consommé Double au Fumet de Tomates.

Truite-Saumonée Norvégienne sur Socle.

Noisettes d'Agneau à l'Estragon.
Petits Pois à la Française.

Caneton de Rouen à l'Ancienne (froid).

Ortolans en Cocotte.
Salade Cœurs de Laitues.

Asperges d'Argenteuil, Sauce Mousseline.

Pêches et Fraises Rafraîchies au St. Marceaux.

May 20th, 1901.

SAVOY HOTEL.

2

Savoy Theatre.

R. D'OYLY CARTE
SOLE PROPRIETOR AND MANAGER.

UTOPIA (LIMITED)
OR
The Flowers of Progress.

An Original Comic Opera,

Written by W. S. Gilbert,
Composed by ARTHUR SULLIVAN.

3

Js/1/. /1902

4

THE
SAVOY
RESTAURANT.

4 & 5. *Menu, Britain, 1901. The folded outer card for the Savoy restaurant menu remains standard, while the inner printed menu was interchangeable.*

5

· MENU ·

Royal Natives.

Poule-au-Pot.
Bisque d'Ecrevisses.

Turbotin à la Boitel.

Poularde Suprême à la Diva.

Selle de Pré-Salé à la Broche.
Petits Pois aux Laitues.
Pommes Fondantes.

Punch à la Romaine.

Grouse à la Broche.

Salade.

Fonds d'Artichauts au Gratin.

Soufflé Café et Pistaches.

Ananas Glacé.
Friandises.
Corbeille de Fruits.

SEPTEMBER 19th, 1901.

6

BANQUET
TO·INAUGURATE·
THE·EXHIBITON·OF
WORKS·OF·MODERN
GERMAN·ARTISTS
AT·THE
LOUIS·XVI
ROOMS
SAVOY
HOTEL
TUESDAY·MAY·22·1906

1. *Menu card, Britain, 1904. A personalized menu with hand-tinted illustrations.*

2 & 3. Utopia Limited or The Flowers of Progress, *Britain, 1893. The comic opera by Gilbert and Sullivan was produced by Richard D'Oyly Carte at the Savoy Theatre. The sensitively drawn illustration by Havers was integrated with text on both the front and inside of this magnificent first-night programme.*

7

MENU

Barquette Allemande.

Potage Okra.
Purée de pois.

Saumon glacé au Champagne.
Concombres Vinaigrette.

Baron de Béhague à la broche Sauce Menthe.
Haricots Verts Lyonnaite.
Pommes nouvelles.

Zéphir à la Monselet.

Poulet reine en Casserole.
Salade Romaine.

Asperges d'argenteuil Sauce Mousseline.

Bombe aux fraises.
Corbeille de friandises

Canapes Edouard VII.

TOASTS

The King.
PROPOSED BY THE CHAIRMAN, THE RT. HON. R. B. HALDANE, M.P.

H.I.M. The Emperor of Germany.
PROPOSED BY THE CHAIRMAN.

Art. Literature. Drama.
PROPOSED BY THE CHAIRMAN.

Reply:
Art.—PROFESSOR VON HERKOMER, R.A.
Literature.—MR. EDMUND GOSSE, LL.D.
Drama.—MR. BERNARD SHAW.

Decorative Art.
PROPOSED BY WALTER CRANE, R.W.S.
REPLY. PROFESSOR VAN DE VELDE.

Our Guests the German Artists.
PROPOSED BY G. W. ROTHENSTEIN.
REPLY. PROFESSOR MAX SLEVOGT.

Visitors.
PROPOSED BY JOHN M. SWAN, R.A.
REPLY. { COUNT KESSLER.
        { HON. GEORGE PEEL.

The Chairman.
PROPOSED BY HERR VON STUMM,
GERMAN CHARGÉ D'AFFAIRES.

6 & 7. *Menu, Britain, 1906. A menu design that does justice to the distinguished guest list. The cover layout incorporates illustration and text in a stylish, inventive manner, using colour as a punctuation device. The list of speakers includes Walter Crane and George Bernard Shaw.*

45

Invitation to fashion show, Britain, c. 1930. Designed by
Edward McKnight Kauffer.

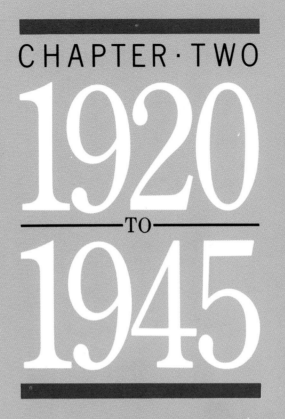

CHAPTER · TWO
1920 TO 1945

INTRODUCTION

After the devastation and loss of life of World War I, Europe was in no mood to continue with the frivolous behaviour that had characterized the immediate pre-war years. The real 20th century can be said to begin in 1918.

New Ideas in Art

The war years heralded a change in the arts. The newly formed Soviet Union led the way, shedding its bourgeois Russian past and its obsession with historic images. Russian artists in all fields, from Vladimir Tatlin's new conception of architectural monuments and the growth of Constructivism, to the group of artists named the Suprematists, were involved in the creation of an identity that could accurately express the concept of the People's State. Art now performed the practical function of serving the people.

Artists such as Vassily Kandinsky, Kasimir Malevich and El Lissitzky involved themselves in the creation of designs, from packaging to posters. They even devised new typestyles, which influenced the layout of books and magazines. Marinetti's First Futurist Manifesto, published in 1909, had given rise to Futurism, the basis of many of the new design ideas developing in Russia.

At the same time, pockets of revolutionary artists were active throughout Europe. In Switzerland, in 1916, the Dada movement emerged as a protest against the folly of the War, and, as an anti-art movement, it ran parallel with the events taking place in Russia. Dada, which means "hobby-horse", caused upheaval in a society that had been visually conditioned before the War. One of its major events was staged in Cologne in 1920; it was held in the back of a café, which was approached via a public lavatory. The guests were invited to destroy the exhibits, and they relished the opportunity to make such a sensational statement by carrying out the wishes of the artists. Simultaneously, new ideas were being developed in Holland and in England, where, respectively, the De Stijl and Vorticist movements were emerging. De Stijl took its name from a Dutch magazine, *De Stijl*, which was edited by Theo van Doesburg, a painter and writer. Van Doesburg (1883-1931) was greatly influenced by Mondrian's simple and geometric approach to the layout of shapes within a space, and he tried to apply the principles to interior design and architecture. The magazine set the style for new commercial art in Europe, influencing posters, packaging and layout. It also had a profound effect on Walter Gropius, the architect and founder of the Bauhaus movement. In England, Percy Wyndham Lewis (1884-1957), a painter and writer, founded Vorticism, which was derived from Cubism and Futurism, and he edited the movement's magazine, *Blast*, which appeared in 1914-15.

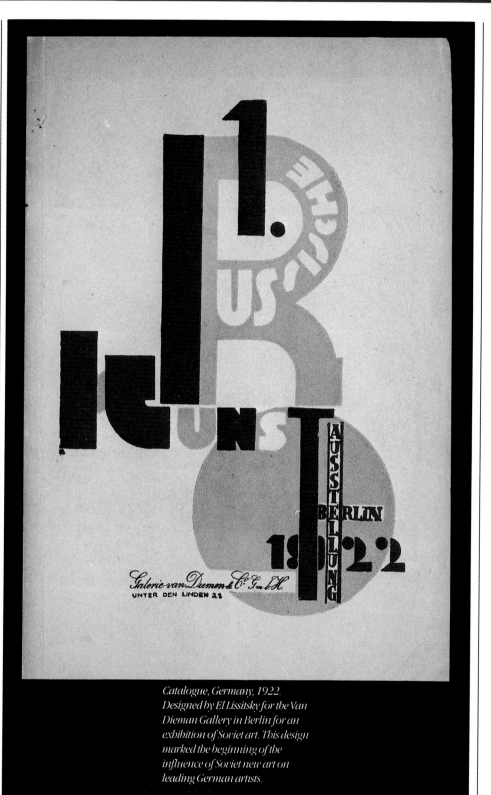

Catalogue, Germany, 1922. Designed by El Lissitsky for the Van Dieman Gallery in Berlin for an exhibition of Soviet art. This design marked the beginning of the influence of Soviet new art on leading German artists.

Lewis believed that art should reflect the complexity of the modern world.

The Bauhaus

In 1919 a momentous event in the history of design occurred in the German town of Weimar, a traditional centre of the arts. Walter Gropius (1883-1969) established the Bauhaus, the first and most influential industrial design school, an action that was to affect every aspect of modern design in the 20th century. Some of Europe's foremost artists – Paul Klee, Johannes Itten, Vassily Kandinsky, Oskar Schlemmer and László Moholy-Nagy, for instance – worked and taught at the Bauhaus in Weimar and, later, at Dessau, attempting to come to terms with the problems of the new machine age. Every aspect of modern living was scrutinized. Designs for functional furniture to be made by machines were produced; houses and offices were designed to accommodate the needs of the people occupying them; and type and layout were developed to serve the modern working society. Herbert Bayer (b. 1900) established the graphic design and advertising section of the Bauhaus, where the study of visual communication and publicity material evolved alongside designs for manufacturing.

The significance of the Bauhaus movement was its insistence on a solid foundation in the philosophy of design, which manifested itself in the movement's permanence and continuation as an influential and established centre of excellence for the teaching of

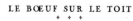

Bon Temp, France, c.1920. This design encapsulates both the fashions of the day and the images that were changing fine art, such as the powerful Cubist movement.

design. Whereas different movements in the arts in Europe fluctuated, deviated and, finally, disappeared, Bauhaus influences continued to be seen in the creation of mass-produced design.

New Ideas and Old Periodicals

The conflict between the appearance of the publications of this period reflects the different philosophies of art that were prevalent in Europe in the immediate post-war period.

A comparison of the two magazines, the German *Der Querschnitt* and the English *Strand*, reveals the differences between the modern thinking and established principles. *Der Querschnitt*, which was founded by Stefan Lorant, was heavily influenced by the emergent Surrealist movement, which allowed the visual subconscious to dominate visual expression. The hugely successful *Strand* magazine, on the other hand, represented a staid and traditional formality.

The importance of the emerging modern ideas, as embodied in *Der Querschnitt*, cannot be underestimated. This magazine was the first in a line of new, important publications. *Lilliput*, the English equivalent, was also founded by Lorant, who took up residence in England and brought with him the new ideas from the Continent of Europe. The format of these magazines also reflected the changed lifestyle of their audience. Their pocket-sized proportions made for comfortable reading while commuters were travelling to office or factory.

Catalogue, Britain, 1934. An exhibition of Zero's (Hans Schleger) work, organized by Lund Humphries. This exhibition marked the beginning of a career that was to influence many other designers. The layout and illustrative components, and the techniques used to display these, are unquestionably ahead of their time.

This exhibition should do much to popularise Zero's work in this country JUST as he must be given credit for past innovations, so may his later work provide stimulus for further progress in modern design, advertising, printing and typography

LUND HUMPHRIES

INTRODUCTION

These magazines were the first to unite photographic images with the written word in a page layout. Lorant's fascination with photography and his recognition of the camera's significance in recording events in a dramatic and meaningful way led to his later formation of the magazine *Picture Post*, itself a landmark in magazine design and concept.

Post-War Publishing

In England, John Lane's Bodley Head, which had led the publishing world with its revolutionary arts review, *The Yellow Book*, was struggling to compete with the changes taking place in post-war society, but John Lane's nephew, Allen Lane, created a new concept in book publishing in 1935. Other leading publishing houses regarded with derision his notion of making literature available to the masses by creating a cheaply bound, small format publication. The idea was not in itself new, but Allen Lane's cunning marketing approach and design awareness provided the mainspring for the successful

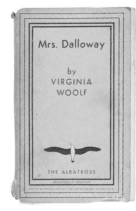

The Albatross, Britain, c.1945. The Albatross design with its sans serif titling, colour coding and the bird colophon had been in use since 1932 and was the basis for the early Penguin range.

Penguin Books. The use of the rather humorous image of a penguin resulted from a visit to London Zoo and led to a flock of successful publishing ventures, including Pelican and Puffin.

Book design in general was undergoing intense scrutiny, and the layout of information was, under the influence of the innovative *Mise en Page*, increasingly a serious subject for review. This experimental book, produced in 1931 by a Parisian printer, A. Tolmer, was created as both an inspiration to, and a criticism of, the work that was currently emerging. Tolmer felt that book design was timid and unstimulating. He set about proving that page layout and design could be interesting, dynamic and full of visual stimuli. Tolmer's inspiration came from the exciting events taking place in the visual arts.

El Lissitzky, whose work appeared in published form, must have been one of the influences in the creation of *Mise en Page*, for his striking new approach to the integration of type with graphic design devices and simple colours broke new ground.

Mise en Page, France, 1931. Published in both French and English this revolutionary book on layout was born out of the new art forms centred in France. It revealed new visual potential in otherwise laboured and sterile layout design. Although the book had only a marginal effect on book layout design, its effect on advertising layout has been immense.

GEBRAUCHSGRAPHIK
INTERNATIONAL ADVERTISING ART

HERAUSGEBER · PROF. H. K. FRENZEL · EDITOR
PHÖNIX ILLUSTRATIONSDRUCK UND VERLAG G. M. B. H. · BERLIN SW 61

Alleinvertreter für die Vereinigten   THE BOOK SERVICE COMPANY   Sole Representative for the United
Staaten von Nordamerika u. Kanada   15 East 40th Street New York City U.S.A   States of America and Canada

*Gebrauchsgraphik, Germany,
1928. Hans Schleger's work took
him to the United States, where his
love of horses and art were
combined in this magnificent
image.*

Typographical Change

In England, Stanley Morison (1889-1967), a student of Edward Johnston, was also breaking new ground in typography at this time. Possibly his most notable work was to redesign *The Times* newspaper in 1932. This was a momentous event in view of *The Times*' staunch resistance to change in the past. Morison believed that newspapers had fallen behind other printed matter in updating their layout and typefaces, and, compared with books, newspaper design did not aid easy reading. It is no coincidence that at the time New Times Roman typeface was being developed, radio was stealing newspaper audiences with its up-to-the-minute news bulletins. To survive in the world of new technology, printed information needed to sell itself visually in a competitive market.

Eric Gill (1882-1940) was another important figure in the presentation of the written word. His revolutionary new sans serif typeface, Gill Sans, showed just how the traditional typefaces were making way for innovative, modern-looking styles.

Not all type styles were so functional and practical as Times New Roman and Gill Sans, however. Fashions in typography reflected a frivolous period in which Hollywood was beginning to dictate fashions and the Charleston was the most popular dance. Broadway, designed by M. F. Benton, was one outcome of this new climate and Bifur, designed by the multi-talented A. M. Cassandre, reflected the style of New York buildings and Art Deco design, and so typified the cross-fertilization of style and art that was everywhere evident.

Germany and World War II

Meanwhile in Germany the Nazis' concern for the purity of German culture extended as far as the re-establishment of German typography, and they insisted that the traditional styles of the Fatherland, black Gothic type, should replace what were seen as decadent styles that had been influenced by Communism on Germany's eastern borders. Extreme pressure was brought to bear on the Bauhaus to make it conform with the Nazi Party's ideals, but its coexistence with the new regime proved impossible. In 1933 it was disbanded, and most of its teachers fled to more sympathetic and accommodating political climates, joining artists of all disciplines from all parts of Europe in their flight from the imminent war.

The advent of war brought about a serious review of the ways in which information was communicated. Art and design were now bound up in the communication of succinct and well-executed messages.

INFLUENCES

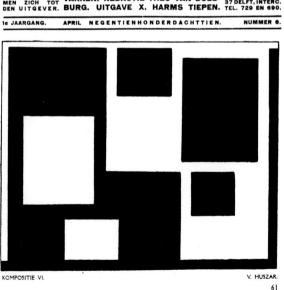

1. For the Voice, *USSR, 1923.
Designed by El Lissitzky, poems by
Mayakovski. Each page layout was
designed by El Lissitzky and set up
in such a way that each poem had
its own index for easy reference. In
selecting a printer who would
follow his revolutionary layout
instructions, Lissitzky ensured
that his work would have a
lasting influence.*

3

2 & 3 De Stijl, *Holland, 1918. Van
Doesburg's approach to layout
clearly influenced the ideas
developing in the Bauhaus. The
geometric forms which aim at unity
and balance evolved into three-
dimensional ideas as shown in this
building from around 1929.*

2

4

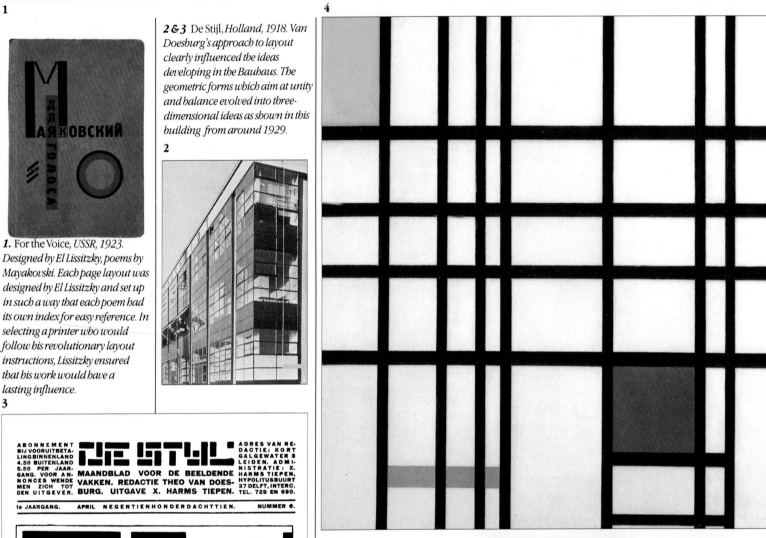

4. Composition with Red, Yellow
and Blue, *France, c.1940. This late
work by Mondrian shows the
clearly defined and positive
geometric approach which evolved
from his earlier association with
van Doesburg.*

5. Head No. 2, *France, 1916.
Sculpture by Naum Gabo. Made
from Cor-Ten steel, this represents
the new art form where images
reflect technological progress and
art embodies the spirit of this new
revolutionary age.*

6

7

7. *Tomb paintings, Egypt, c.1300 BC. The discovery of Tutankhamen's tomb had an impact worldwide on all that was visual.*

6. Gazette du bon ton, *France, 1921. Gouache by Berbier illustrating an evening dress by Worth. Even ladies' fashions appeared to echo the refined linear shape found in art and* architecture. Egyptian art and the new discoveries of tombs were also influential in the graphic style of the period.

9. *Mise en Page, France, 1931. A publication on layout design that influenced at least two decades.*

8. *Car, Germany, c.1929. The advances in technology now combined power, practicality and styling. The balance of beautifully* proportioned geometric form influenced lifestyle and set the tone for a new modern approach to art and technology.

MAGAZINES

1

2

3

HUMOUR

By Roda Roda

Hassan the Pious

THERE once lived a man called Hassan, who was famed far and wide for his piety. He had devoted his life to study, and was so wrapped up in his books that he did not notice that his relatives were robbing him. Almost a greybeard, he was suddenly confronted with poverty.

But Hassan did not despair. He knew that even if the wicked ones had taken his treasure, he owned a jewel of which no one could rob him—his reputation. And he decided to put this to good use.

He went to the market-place, spread his carpet and cried:

"Hearken to me, good people all who may be plagued with toothache! I, Hassan the Pious, will cure you through my prayers."

Soon all the sufferers from the neighbourhood came to be healed.

When someone came and complained, Hassan first blessed him, then strode three times round him, threw himself three times on his carpet, blessed him again three times, walked round him and threw himself seven times to the ground;

blessed him again and laid his hand on his forehead; at last he drew an enormous pair of pincers from his robe, a terrifying implement.

Then he asked the patient:

"Do your teeth still hurt?"

"No," was the invariable reply. And the people around were astounded, and murmured words of praise and lauded Hassan's piety.

One day, a man with a very swollen face pushed his way through the crowds.

"Hurry up," he said to Hassan, "I am in terrible pain."

Hassan raised his hands and began to bless the man. But the stranger waved him aside.

"Hurry up, I told you, I'm in agony."

"Patience, dear friend," mildly answered Hassan. "Patience and you will be cured." And he raised his hands again.

But the stranger became furious.

"Hurry, Hassan, I command you and take your pincers! For I tell you, I am Ebul Fidas, the pious man of Jaffa, and I also cure my patients by my piety!"

IS THIS THE NEW ART?
The Comfortable Seat
Surrealist furniture designed by Kurt Seligmann

4

1 & 2. Der Querschnitt, *Germany, 1932. Heavily influenced by Surrealist images, the cover illustration and inside photography display a witty and intellectual humour. The photographs and copy are geometrically laid out on the pages.* *3 & 4.* Lilliput, *Britain, 1938.* Lilliput *covers by Walter Trier always included a boy, a girl and a dog.* Lilliput *was founded by Stefan Lorant, using ideas from his pre-Nazi* Der Querschnitt. *Comparing these pages from* Lilliput *and* Der Querschnitt *shows how the philosophy and style was continued in the British publication.* *5 & 6.* The Sphere, *Britain, 1933. This large-format magazine, using two broad columns, continued a tradition*

5

6

7

8

9

10

from earlier arts magazines.
Note the adventurous use of
illustrations breaking into the
columns of copy.

7 & 8. Punch, Britain, 1939.
The Richard Doyle cover was not
used in special issues such as the
Autumn number shown here.
The layout of the magazine was
formal and several grids with
different numbers of columns
were used. The magazine relied
heavily on the works of satirical
illustrators to punctuate the
wordy pages.

9 & 10. The Illustrated London
News, Britain, 1934. This
commemorative number shows
the continuation of the tradition
of using illustrations to depict
significant events. This formula
was used before the journalistic
use of photography and
continued beyond the date of
this publication. The layout
design is formal and dignified,
and is enhanced by the subtle use
of tints of colour.

MAGAZINES

1. L'Esprit Nouveau, *France, c.1920. The styling of this international arts review reflects the manifestos of the time.*
2. Saturday Evening Post, *USA, 1936. The illustration and type have been integrated in this commemorative issue.*
3. Industrial Arts, *Britain, 1936. A modern magazine, supporting the collaboration of the arts and industry.*
4 & 5. The Strand Magazine, *Britain, 1923/1929. Established in 1891, this developed into the most popular magazine of its time, the exciting and stimulating copy integrated with illustration.*

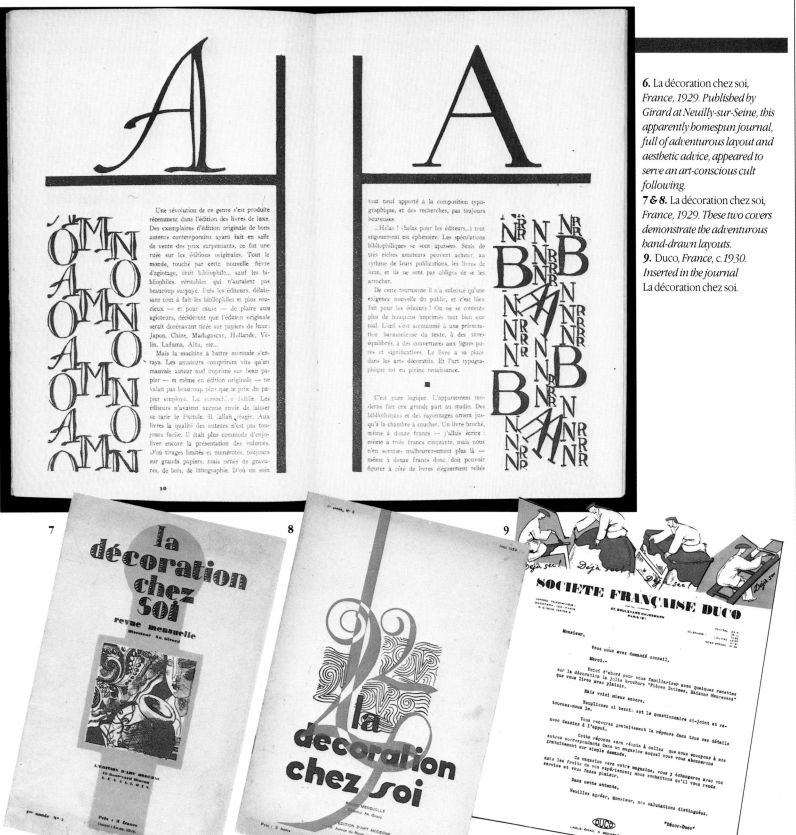

6. La décoration chez soi, *France, 1929. Published by Girard at Neuilly-sur-Seine, this apparently homespun journal, full of adventurous layout and aesthetic advice, appeared to serve an art-conscious cult following.*

7 & 8. La décoration chez soi, *France, 1929. These two covers demonstrate the adventurous hand-drawn layouts.*

9. Duco, *France, c.1930. Inserted in the journal* La décoration chez soi.

BOOKS

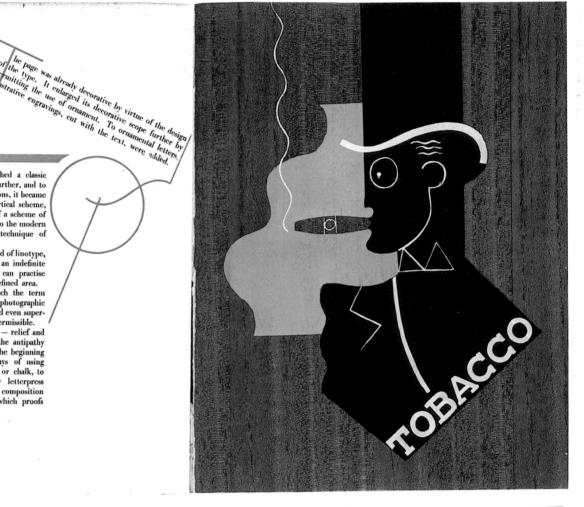

This rectilinear arrangement has established a classic standard of lay-out. In order to go a step further, and to obtain a greater variety of possible combinations, it became necessary to abandon the horizontal and vertical scheme, or at all events to develop the alternative of a scheme of obliques and curves. At this point we come to the modern technique, and more particularly to the technique of modern advertising.

Henceforward, whether dealing with the lead of linotype, or the mould of a whole page from which an indefinite number of impressions are required, one can practise every freedom of composition within the defined area.

In the process involving intaglio, to which the term photogravure is applied in reference to its photographic origin, the free and intimate juxtaposition and even super-imposition of type and illustrations is permissible.

Apart from the two main forms of printing — relief and intaglio — lithography, which is based on the antipathy between greasy inks and water, appeared at the beginning of the XIXth. century. The different ways of using lithography, from direct drawing with ink or chalk, to the transfer of proofs obtained either by letterpress or copperplate, permit great freedom in the composition of the page, thanks to the facility with which proofs can be transferred on the stone.

The page was already decorative by virtue of the design of the type. It enlarged its decorative scope further by permitting the use of ornament. To ornamental letters, illustrative engravings, cut with the text, were added.

1. Mise en Page, *English edition, 1931. This book, packed with photo-montage and lively illustration, had a long-lasting influence on the layout work produced in advertising agencies in America, France and England.*

2, 3 & 4. Book jackets, Britain, 1937. A variety of styles ranging from a completely illustrative use of type and image, to the decorative layout of type and graphic devices used in* Sandbar Sinister, *a typical Gollancz book.*

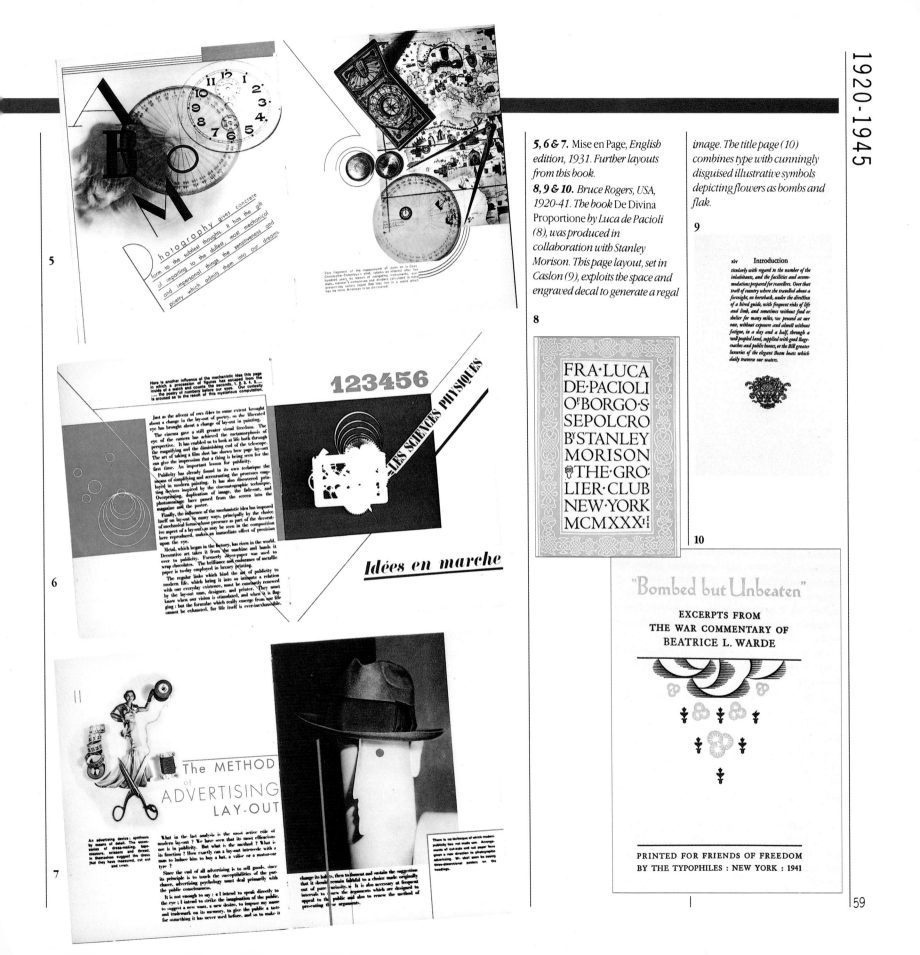

5, 6 & 7. Mise en Page, *English edition, 1931. Further layouts from this book.*

8, 9 & 10. *Bruce Rogers, USA, 1920-41. The book* De Divina Proportione *by Luca de Pacioli (8), was produced in collaboration with Stanley Morison. This page layout, set in Caslon (9), exploits the space and engraved decal to generate a regal image. The title page (10) combines type with cunningly disguised illustrative symbols depicting flowers as bombs and flak.*

BOOKS

1. The Fast Lady, *Britain, c. 1925. Designed by Nick. The colour coordination between the illustration and type is especially good.*

2 & 3. Die Geschichte des Manon Lescaut, *Germany, 1920. Published by Insel Verlag, Leipzig. The delicate line border incorporates* drawings reminiscent of Beardsley. *Note the restrained and subtle use of a lemon tint and red on the title page.*

2

1

3

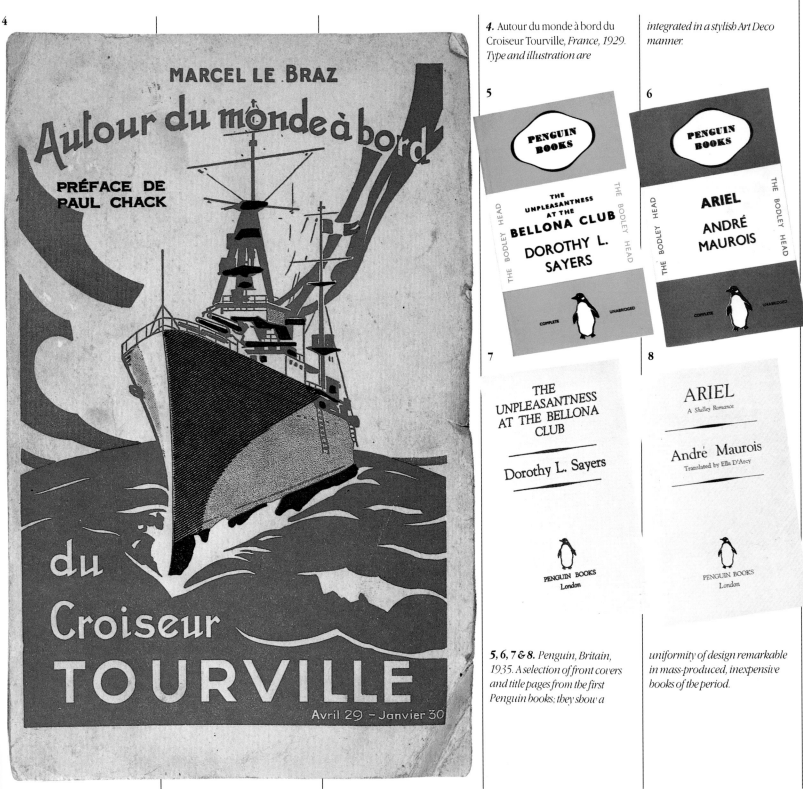

4. Autour du monde à bord du Croiseur Tourville, *France, 1929. Type and illustration are* integrated *in a stylish Art Deco manner.*

5, 6, 7 & 8. *Penguin, Britain, 1935. A selection of front covers and title pages from the first Penguin books; they show a* uniformity *of design remarkable in mass-produced, inexpensive books of the period.*

CHILDREN'S BOOKS

1 & 2. Mon Histoire de France, *France, c.1920. This splendid condensed history with beautiful engraved illustrations, and set in a traditional, elegant Bodoni typeface, is a fine example of the quality printing and layout of the period.*

3. Les Deux Coqs, *France, c.1930. Illustrated by Claude Garnier. Even in the most humble publications, design and layout were carefully considered.*

1

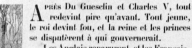

2

3

4

5

4, 5, 6 & 7.
Philippe chez les Sauvages,
*France, 1934. Illustrated and
designed by Jacques Viotte, this
hand-printed book combines the
layout and display of type in an
integrated form as shown in the
first inside page.*

6

PHILIPPE CHEZ LES SAUVAGES

PHILIPPE
CHEZ LES
SAUVAGES

PHILIPPE
ÉTAIT   TROP
PETIT   ENCORE
POUR   ALLER
EN   BATEAU.

IL VIT UN GRAND NOMBRE DE HUTTES
DISPOSÉES EN CERCLE AUTOUR D'UN
POTEAU DE FORME BIZARRE; MAIS LE
CAMPEMENT SEMBLAIT ABANDONNÉ.

APRÈS AVOIR
MANGÉ QUELQUES
BANANES POUR
APAISER UN PEU
SA FAIM, IL VIT
QUE LA NUIT
COMMENÇAIT A
TOMBER.
IL ENTENDIT
DES CRIS DE BÊTES
SAUVAGES DANS
LA FORÊT ET
POUR SE METTRE
A L'ABRI, IL
S'INSTALLA SUR
LE POTEAU ET
S'Y ENDORMIT.

7

NEW TYPEFACES

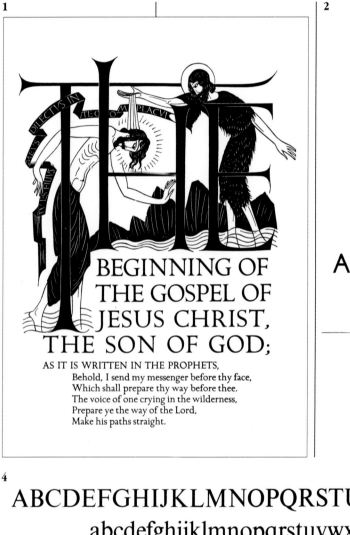

BEGINNING OF THE GOSPEL OF JESUS CHRIST, THE SON OF GOD;

AS IT IS WRITTEN IN THE PROPHETS,
Behold, I send my messenger before thy face,
Which shall prepare thy way before thee.
The voice of one crying in the wilderness,
Prepare ye the way of the Lord,
Make his paths straight.

ABCDEFGHIJKLMNOPQRSTUVWXYZ
abcdefghijklmnopqrstuvwxyz
1234567890

ABCDEFGHIJKLMNOPQRSTUVWXYZ
abcdefghijklmnopqrstuvwxyz
1234567890

ABCDEFGHIJKLMNOPQRSTUVWXYZ
1234567890

❡ The Lanston Monotype Machine Company has given to Bruce Rogers permission to print for himself two hundred and twenty-three copies of this pamphlet on hand-made paper at the Press of William Edwin Rudge Mt. Vernon New York
M D C
CCC
XX
IV
✳
✳
✳

ABCDEFGHIJKLMNOPQRSTUVWXYZ
abcdefghijklmnopqrstuvwxyz
1234567890
ABCDEFGHIJKLMNOPQRSTUVWXYZ
abcdefghijklmnopqrstuvwxyz
1234567890

1. Beginning of Mark's Gospel, Britain, c.1930. Designed and illustrated by Eric Gill (1882-1940).
2. Gill Sans, Gill Sans medium, *Britain, c.1930. Designed by Eric Gill and influenced by Edward Johnston's railway letter forms.*
3. Pamphlet, USA, 1924. Designed by Bruce Rogers.
4. Times New Roman, Britain, 1931. Designed for The Times newspaper by Stanley Morison.

5

KÖRPER
UND STIMME
LEIHT DIE SCHRIFT
DEM STUMMEN
GEDANKEN
DURCH
DER
JAHRHUNDERTE
STROM
TRÄGT IHN
DAS
REDENDE BLATT

6

MÄRZ

Donnerstag	1	Albinus
Freitag	2	Luise
Samstag	3	Kunigunde
SONNTAG	4	3. Oculi
Montag	5	Friedrich
Dienstag	6	Fridolin
Mittwoch	7	Felizitas
Donnerstag	8	Philemon
Freitag	9	Franziska
Samstag	10	Henriette
SONNTAG	11	4. Lätare
Montag	12	Gregor P.
Dienstag	13	Ernst
Mittwoch	14	Mathilde
Donnerstag	15	Isabella
Freitag	16	Heribert
Samstag	17	Gertrud
SONNTAG	18	5. Judica
Montag	19	Joseph
Dienstag	20	Eugen
Mittwoch	21	Benedikt
Donnerstag	22	Nikolaus
Freitag	23	Eberhard
Samstag	24	Bertha
SONNTAG	25	Mariä Verk.
Montag	26	Emanuel
Dienstag	27	Rupert
Mittwoch	28	Priskus
Donnerstag	29	Gründonnerst.
Freitag	30	Karfreitag
Samstag	31	Balbina

FRÜHLING

7. *Title page, Germany, 1926. Behrens Antiqua was designed by Peter Behrens (1869-1940), who was also responsible for the renowned logo for AEG.*

5. *Text in Koch Antiqua, Germany, c.1926. Also known as Locarno, it was originally designed for Klingspor in 1922.*

6. *Calendar, Germany, c.1926. Two pages from* Klingspor Kalender *in Koch Antiqua, designed by W. Harweth.*

7

ALFRED LICHTWARK
DIE GRUNDLAGEN
DER KÜNSTLERISCHEN
BILDUNG

STUDIEN
AUS DEN VORTRÄGEN
AN DER HAMBURGER
KUNSTHALLE

BAND I-III
Die Seele und das Kunstwerk
Die Erziehung des Farbensinnes
Palastfenster und Flügeltür
1926

VERLAG BRUNO CASSIRER · BERLIN

INFLUENCE OF PHOTOGRAPHY

1, 2, 3 & 4. Weekly Illustrated, *Britain, 1935. An early example of photographic reportage, in which photography played a major part in the visual layout. This souvenir edition for George V's jubilee shows the inventive use of photography in depicting a visual story.*

5, 6 & 7. Match, *France, 1939. A forerunner of* Paris Match, *which was established in 1949,* Match *pioneered photography as a dramatic means of depicting current events. The weight and shape of layout is governed by the tonal contrast of photographs.*

INFLUENCE OF PHOTOGRAPHY

1, 2 & 3. Picture Post, *Britain, 1941. This publication was created by Stefan Lorant, after* Der Querschnitt *and* Lilliput. *Throughout its existence it employed photographers such as Bert Hardy, Kurt Hutton and Leonard McCombe.*

Picture Post, January 4, 1941

THE TWO SYSTEMS OF EDUCATION: *A Picture That Sums Up Our Main Problem*
Two boys stand top-hatted outside Lord's cricket ground. Three boys stand bare-headed and stare at them. Between the two groups is a barrier—deliberately created by our system of education. Our task is to remove the barrier—to bring the public schools into the general scheme.

A PLAN FOR EDUCATION

by A. D. Lindsay

Author is Master of Balliol College, Oxford. He has been there since 1924. University men look up to him as an outstanding teacher and administrator. One of the leaders of progress in educational ideas.

THE things most obviously wrong with English education to-day in my opinion are :—

(1) There is still, on the whole, one system of education for the poor and another for the rich.

(2) For the poor, education ends at too early an age.

(3) The conditions under which boys from the primary school can climb the educational ladder to the Universities are such that we are paying for a great blessing—democracy in the universities—with a new curse—the production of an intelligentsia in the worst sense of that term.

(4) The excessive specialisation of our higher secondary and university education is producing the same effect.

I should like, as a corrective background of these criticisms, to say that the great advantage of the English educational system is its variety and

WHAT WE WANT

- *The same kind of education for all up to the age of 13.*
- *"Educative control" for all up to the age of 18.*
- *The child's future education to be decided at 13.*
- *The public schools brought into the general system.*
- *Some Youth Service for everybody.*
- *A break between secondary school and University.*
- *An overhaul of the curriculum in Universities.*

adaptability—if you like, its unsystematic character, its happy mingling of statutory and voluntary organisation. I hope we shall resist all attempts to make our education over-tidy.

This is important to bear in mind when we consider the first of the evils I have mentioned—the fact that there is in this country one system of education for the poor and another for the rich. For we might try to cure that evil by saying that there should only be one system of education for everybody. But the great variety of types of secondary schools in this country—from the public schools at the one end to technical schools at the other—is not an evil. The evil is a different one. The decision as to which boys should go to which schools, or be trained in which system, depends not on ability or fitness, but on wealth and class. The social division thus created is the outstanding evil.

2

WORK FOR ALL
By Thomas Balogh

3

PICTURE POST

HULTON'S NATIONAL WEEKLY A PLAN FOR BRITAIN JANUARY 4, 1941 3D

4, 5 & 6. Signal, *English edition,* 1943. The formal, four-column layout of this German propaganda magazine is used to give importance to the page, which cleverly integrates both sentimental and industrial photographic images.

COMICS

1. Ovaltiney's Own Comic, *Britain, 1936. Linked to the famous product as a device for promotion and entertainment, the conventional layout is lifted out of the ordinary by the novel lettering used as a heading.*

2, 3 & 4. The Magnet, *Britain, 1937. A wordy and responsible publication, it was laid out in a rather formal, intimidating manner for such a young audience. The inside spreads, based on a three-column grid, are densely packed with vital information. The main visual relief comes from the pages of advertisements, which promote responsible and serious hobbies.*

5 & 6. Mickey Mouse Weekly, *English edition, 1938. This American publication makes the English comics look positively antique. Its striking use of colour and energetic layout combine to provide stimulating and exciting reading for its young audience.*

LIFESTYLE MAGAZINES

1 & 2. Harper's Bazaar, *USA, 1932.*
3. McCall's, *USA, 1936.*
4. Vogue, *Britain, 1936.*
5. Modern Publicity, *Britain, 1930. An early example of modern, unconventional layout in which curved backgrounds and montaged photographs are brought together with text in a new layout format.*

1

WOOLENS IN A
STELLAR RÔLE

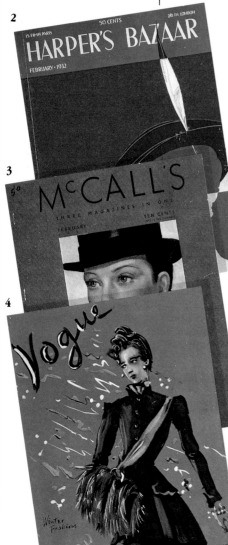

2

3

4

5

6 & 7. Modern Woman, *Britain, 1937. A popular magazine of the time. Spot colour is used sparingly but to great effect.* **8 & 9.** Gazette du bon ton, *France, c.1921.*

TRAVEL INFORMATION

1. *Identification label, France, c.1920. This highly decorative design adorned the luggage of well-to-do travellers.*

2 & 3. Riva Torbole, *Italy, 1937. A layout using montage and selective colour images to personalize the holiday on offer. The stylish front cover illustration by Romoli integrates the fashionable new style typography with an elegant layout.*
4. *Identification label, USA, c.1920.*

LES AUTOSTRADES EN ITALIE

VISIT THE USSR

SAVOY HOTEL LONDON

LONDON · IS · NEARER

toutes les autostrades qui se dirigent vers les Lacs. A Laïnate, se détache un embranchement qui mène à Côme: 24 km. 507 mètres, presque en ligne droite, sont parcourus comme dans un éclair et

le touriste se trouve à CÔME, petite ville admirablement située et remarquable par ses monuments, dont le plus important est la Cathédrale. Une fois à Côme, on peut faire en bateau une délicieuse excursion sur le LAC, l'un des plus pittoresques de la Péninsule à cause mê-

me de sa configuration géographique, de sa végétation, des localités et des villas qui animent ses bords. Le tronçon Laïnate-Gallarate conduit, en 20 km. 673, à cette industrieuse petite ville de laquelle se détachent deux embranchements. L'un, d'une longueur de 11 km. 119 conduit à Sesto Calende. L'autre, de 16 km. 235, mène à Varèse: Sesto Calende est presque aux abords du LAC MAJEUR, lac d'une

5 & 6. Les Autostrades en Italie, France, 1935. A dynamic and forceful layout incorporating illustration and type, but the concern to impose the layout of the design is unsympathetic to the text, which is almost unreadable.
7. Visit the USSR, USA, c. 1930. A montage of illustration featuring the new style of Russian design in both illustration and type.

8 & 9. Savoy Hotel, Britain, 1938. Some adventurous publicity material was designed to encourage the London tourist trade. No explanation is needed on the exquisitely visual spread.

1

GALES, HURRICANES, TYPHOONS, WATERFALLS, tides, Atlantic rollers, geysers and volcanoes. Forest trees are flung down. Cliffs are undercut and fall into the sea. Volcanic explosions spout dust and stones miles into the air. These forces run to waste Engineers have contrived methods of disciplining such forces and using them to drive machines. The link between these forces and the machine is the lever. The sails of a windmill and the paddles of a water-wheel and the crank of a steam engine are levers. Only by levers can natural forces—like the power of expanding steam or exploding petrol vapour—be made to drive machines The simplest kind of lever is a crow-bar. It is a bar pivoted nearer one end than the other. By pressing down the end of the long arm you can raise a weight on the end of the short arm, which you could not lift by yourself. And the longer the part of the lever you are pressing on, and

7

2

ARTHUR ELTON

THE
SELF CHANGING
OR
PRE-SELECTIVE
EPICYCLIC
GEAR

3

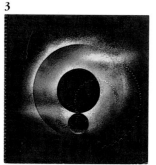

1 & 2. Shell, Britain, c. 1935. Designed by Hans Schleger to announce a major development, this was considered by the client to be a stunning approach to communicating a complex concept to the public. The title page uses a number of interesting devices to give perspective and depth to the information on display.
3. Shell, Britain, c. 1935. The cover design echoes the styling used for the page layouts, and the spine for this book is characteristic of Hans Schleger's work with this type of binding.
4. HMSO, Britain, World War II and after. A distinctly official appearance gives a memorable image to these otherwise functional documents.

4

ON HIS MAJESTY'S SERVICE
OFFICIAL PAID

Your
Ration Book
Issued to safeguard your food supply

Name
Address

NATIONAL REGISTRATION NUMBER

Date of Issue   Serial Number of Book

If found, please return to: BX 481952

FOOD OFFICE   R.B.1 (General)

NATIONAL
REGISTRATION

NATIONAL
REGISTRATION
IDENTITY
CARD
WITH ENDORSEMENT (POLICE)

SUPPLEMENT TO RADIO TIMES, JANUARY 8, 1937

RADIO TIMES
TELEVISION
SUPPLEMENT

PROGRAMMES FROM JANUARY 11 TO 16

SINCE the beginning of November, the BBC has been giving a regular service of television programmes from the London Television Station at Alexandra Palace. Television is still in its earliest stage; programme hours are limited to two a day, and more people see television in public viewing rooms than in their own homes. There is still much to be learnt at the transmitting end; television is only beginning to find a programme technique.

But the coming of television has opened up prospects exciting even in this age of scientific marvels. Those who are following its growth are seeing the development of an amazing extension of human powers, the end of which we can hardly foresee. They can watch this development better in Britain than anywhere else, for even in its present stage, the BBC television service is unrivalled anywhere else in the world.

And television is full of human interest. Sound broadcasting has proved how much personality can be conveyed by the voice alone, but the viewer can see the announcer, the speakers, and the singers whom he hears. The studios of Alexandra Palace are as colourful as the backstage of a theatre, and as fascinating as a film studio. Everybody who has seen a television broadcast will want to know more about the people he has seen, about the atmosphere of the studios, and how it is all done.

From this week onwards, the RADIO TIMES will help its readers to keep track of television progress by means of this weekly Television Supplement. It will contain not only television programmes for the week, but news of future arrangements, studies of television personalities, and articles in which the people who are tackling the problems of television at Alexandra Palace will explain their aspirations, their difficulties, and their plans.

In fact the Television Supplement will do for viewers what the RADIO TIMES itself does for listeners. It will give them full BBC programmes and all about them, and make it easy for them to select in advance the programmes that they want to see.

For the present, while Alexandra Palace remains the only television station giving regular programmes in Britain, this Supplement will be included only in the London Edition of the RADIO TIMES. We hope it will be interesting to our readers, and that even those who are not yet viewers will find it a useful means of keeping in touch with a factor that will, sooner or later, affect their everyday lives.

5. Radio Times, *Britain, 1937.*
A symbol of high-technology takes pride of place across this well-engineered page.
6. Ford News, *USA, 1939.*
Corporate publicity took on a stylish tone with the use of specially designed typefaces to give the company a distinctive, modern image.

6

NEWSPAPERS

1. The British Worker, *Britain, 1926. A special newspaper covering the industrial collapse* of the 1926 General Strike was published by the Trades Union Congress.

2. Volkischer Beobachter, *Germany, 1933. Published by Adolf Hitler. The traditional black type was used.*

3. San Francisco Chronicle, *USA, 1941. The publication masthead and the main front page copy were shifted down to accommodate the dramatic announcement.*

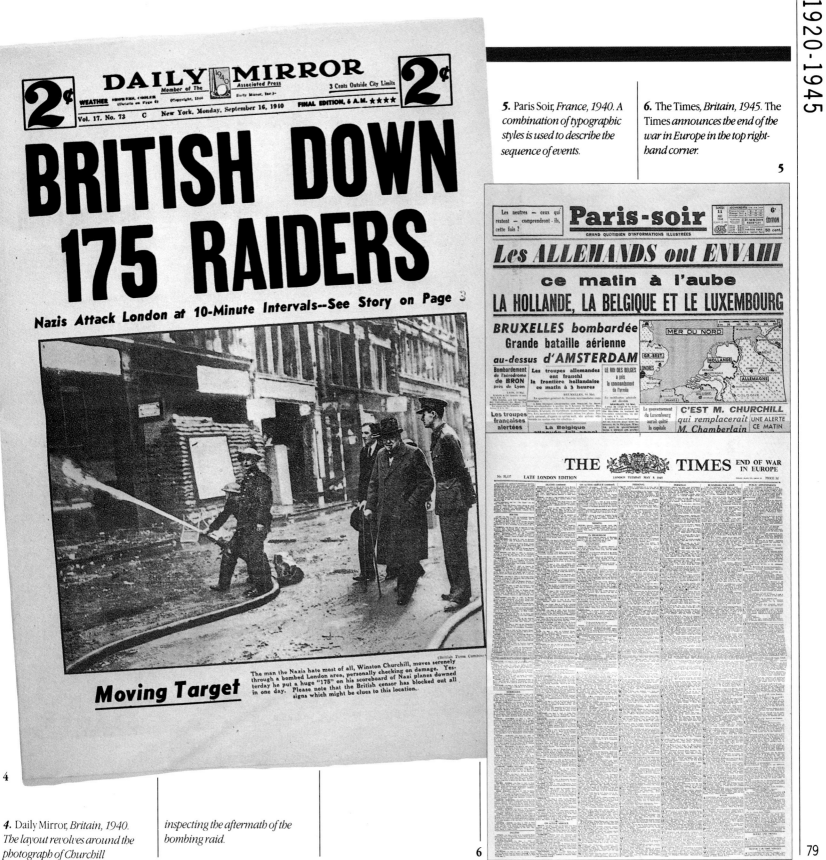

DAILY MIRROR

2¢   2¢

WEATHER   Member of The   Associated Press   3 Cents Outside City Limits

Vol. 17. No. 73   C   New York, Monday, September 16, 1940   FINAL EDITION, 6 A.M. ★★★★

BRITISH DOWN 175 RAIDERS

Nazis Attack London at 10-Minute Intervals--See Story on Page 3

Moving Target

The man the Nazis hate most of all, Winston Churchill, moves serenely through a bombed London area, personally checking on damage. Yesterday he put a huge "175" on his scoreboard of Nazi planes downed in one day. Please note that the British censor has blocked out all signs which might be clues to this location.

---

5. Paris Soir, *France, 1940. A combination of typographic styles is used to describe the sequence of events.*

6. The Times, *Britain, 1945. The* Times *announces the end of the war in Europe in the top right-hand corner.*

5

Paris-soir

Les neutres — ceux qui restent — comprendront - ils, cette fois ?

GRAND QUOTIDIEN D'INFORMATIONS ILLUSTRÉES

Les ALLEMANDS ont ENVAHI
ce matin à l'aube
LA HOLLANDE, LA BELGIQUE ET LE LUXEMBOURG

BRUXELLES bombardée
Grande bataille aérienne
au-dessus d'AMSTERDAM

Bombardement de l'aérodrome de BRON près de Lyon

Les troupes allemandes ont franchi la frontière hollandaise ce matin à 3 heures

LE ROI DES BELGES a pris le commandement de l'armée

Les troupes françaises alertées

C'EST M. CHURCHILL qui remplacerait M. Chamberlain

UNE ALERTE CE MATIN

THE TIMES

END OF WAR IN EUROPE

LATE LONDON EDITION   LONDON TUESDAY MAY 8, 1945

4

4. Daily Mirror, *Britain, 1940. The layout revolves around the photograph of Churchill* inspecting the aftermath of the bombing raid.

6

Typographica, *Britain, 1962, edited by Herbert Spencer
and published by Lund Humphries.*

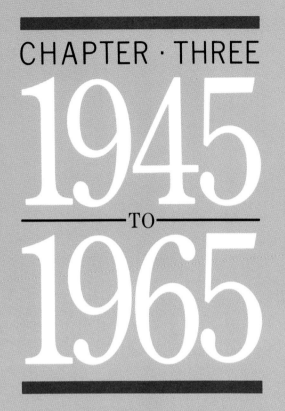

CHAPTER · THREE

1945
TO
1965

INTRODUCTION

World War II prompted many changes in the world of visual arts. When newsreel cameras entered Germany in 1945, the extent of the holocaust and its horrors were recorded on film and displayed to a shocked world. The unbelievable events that had taken place moved artists to the point of despair. In the United States, to which most of Germany's premier artists and designers had been forced to flee, a new art form, the art of self-expression, Abstract Expressionism, became the manifestation of this anger.

Post-War Consumerism

A new generation of artists emerged. Europe, now looking towards America for its inspiration, was still attempting to rebuild itself after the devastation of the war years. Europeans, suffering from shortages of many goods, experienced hardship that transcended thoughts of art. The United States, however, although it was to be involved in wars for most of the 1940s, 1950s and 1960s, was able to develop an expanding and vibrant economy. Its lead in the mass-production of consumer goods enabled it to offer an unprecedented degree of prosperity to its citizens.

Art no longer relied only on a figurative or historic base; instead, experimentation with form and especially

Gas Attack, *Britain, c.1940. In the lean war years, design had a functional utility look, which is clearly visible in this wartime layout.*

colour became characteristic of the period. Artists in Europe were inspired by the frankness of American painters, and by the 1950s young British painters such as Bridget Riley (b. 1931) were exploiting new and complex graphic forms. Paintings became a series of optical elements that created an illusion – a movement that became known as Op (or Optical) Art.

The selling of goods to a demanding and increasingly discerning public became a major force. Consumerism was encouraged by increasingly sophisticated commercial art propaganda, and energetically cultivated by the giant advertising agencies that were increasing day by day in numbers, stature and respectability. Artists involved in the creation of product advertising noted the cultural changes that society was undergoing, and they became aware of the social significance of their commercial work. Andy Warhol (1928-89), for instance, a struggling commercial artist at the time, identified the already-famous label on tins of Campbell's soup and immortalized it by making it a fine art object in the early 1960s. Many similar artists were pursuing their own ideas, generated by the publicity accorded to popular consumerism, and they became the forerunners of the Pop Artists.

Artists and their extreme ideas were shaking the establishment and its set ways. Designers from Europe,

1947 Studebaker Champion Regal De Luxe 4-door Sedan for six passengers.

Studebaker brochure, USA, 1947. The caption to this layout spells out the new thinking and optimism – "A brand new car for a bright new world". America, at this time, set the pace and style of layout design for the consumer society.

Graphis, Switzerland, 1944. The first issue of this design magazine boldly explored the art of Picasso and his contemporaries. In Germany at this time the authorities were condemning such art as decadent.

who had fled to America in the 1930s, had taken with them sophisticated and highly advanced notions of design, and by the early 1950s they were influencing design in America. Moholy-Nagy had established the new Bauhaus in Chicago as early as 1937, and since 1938 Herbert Bayer had worked in New York where he had a marked influence on the design of advertising.

Magazines, aware of the potential of selling lucrative advertising space, began to revise their images in an attempt to encourage advertising agencies to take space on their pages. The powerful grip that editors had always exerted on magazines' content and style was soon loosened by those who were concerned with the magazine's presentation. The role of the typographer/designer became increasingly important, giving scope for leading exponents in the art of layout to become highly paid and respected practitioners of their craft.

Graphic Design Magazines

Graphic artists, to use their new name, were now able to develop their own genre of publications, which went far beyond the scope of those titles that had hitherto served the sector. *Graphis,* a tri-lingual Swiss publication, was launched in 1944 as a showcase for the best in graphic design. It quickly became a reference for designers who wanted to know about developments achieved by their international contemporaries.

Typographica, which was edited by Herbert Spencer, made typography both an art and a practical, functional subject. Its stylish, one-column format, with its wide inner margin, provided a consistent layout for information while allowing great flexibility for the design of images. Dedicated to the review of typography and typographic design, as well as all associated literature, its concern for the design of information even led to a number of articles on reading for the blind being accompanied by printed sheets in Braille.

While *Graphis* covered the glossier developments in design, *Typographica* took a deep look at many long-term factors in specialist areas. For example, by the 1960s Penguin Books had undergone many major design reviews, and in 1962 *Typographica* published an in-depth review of Penguin's progress.

The development of Penguin Books affords a fine example of the changes and trends in layout and design during this period, for it reflects the social, commercial and artistic climate of the age. Edward Young's early jacket design continued to be used until 1947, when Penguin, no doubt aware of the imminent expansion in the quantity of reading matter to be published, enlisted the services of the Swiss typographer Jan Tschichold (1902-74) His work in carefully giving each of the sections of the Penguin empire its own identity established new

guidelines for the reading public. His most effective designs were those for the Penguin Shakespeares, where, curiously, the use of reversed-out type gave them a historic appearance. Tschichold's high standards set a target for designers to follow, and over the next 15 years many distinguished designers, such as Alan Fletcher and Colin Forbes, were engaged in the design of Penguins.

Fine Art and Commercial Design

In America a unique marriage was taking place between the activities of fine artists and those artists working in the commercial design sector. An extremely talented group of designers formed the Push Pin Studios, and by the mid-1950s Push Pin artists were engaged in the design and layout of projects ranging from advertising to publishing. They successfully absorbed the best of the current trends and techniques in fine art and, armed with this knowledge, became a vital force in the commercial art world. Their skill in manipulating colour, illustration and type created a distinctive and powerful style that was imitated throughout Europe.

Zoo Birds, Britain, 1951. The post-war baby boom, together with the advances made in colour printing, saw the beginning of the exquisitely illustrated children's educational books. The layout takes two delicate columns of text and divides them with a flowing arrangement of shaped illustrations.

Many exciting design activities were taking place in America at this time as some of the best-established international magazines were remodelled. In 1955 the Viennese designer, Henry Wolf, who had settled in America in 1941, was art directing and designing for *Esquire* and *Harper's Bazaar*. His reshaping of the layout of both these magazines set the tone for others to follow. By 1959 *McCall's*, under the influence of Otto Storch, had changed its appearance.

As well as changes in the appearance of established magazines, however, this was the time of the new "arty" designer magazines. Herb Lubalin, by now America's foremost designer, was involved in the design of *Eros* and *Avant Garde*, although it must be said that these publications were more noted for their page layout and typographic design than for their financial success.

Pop Music and Design

The American influence on Europe was not limited to the field of design. In 1959 rock-and-roll music, in the shape of Bill Haley, hit Europe. During the immediate post-war years, England, France and the Federal Republic of Germany had been undergoing a massive population explosion, and by the late 1950s a huge market of young people was demanding and creating its own identity. Employment prospects were looking bright and good wages seemed, for the first time, to supply the working sector with surplus money to spend on leisure. American movies, by now presenting glamorous images in a highly sophisticated way, revealed the music and style that shaped a new generation. The 1955 film, *The Blackboard Jungle*, with Bill Haley's "Rock Around the Clock" playing behind the credits, set the youth on two continents alight, and was followed by the well-documented arrival on the scene of a procession of pop heroes, none more significant and influential than the Beatles.

It was, however, some time before the film and music industries had any fundamental impact on the development of graphic layout. The advance in graphics at this time was more in the area of photography, which had natural links with the film and pop industry. By the early 1960s, developments in film and camera technology encouraged art students everywhere to attempt to create photographs that outshone the old masters.

The new generation grew increasingly reliant on the images conveyed through cinema and television. The world was becoming smaller, as filmed images were projected into homes at the push of a button, and magazines, advertising and all forms of graphic information came to rely on the images generated by a new breed of artist/photographer.

The early days of the pop era saw a number of fairly crudely produced publications, such as the *Beatles Monthly*, which, in graphic terms, were unsophisticated and which relied on photographic images to appeal to their teenage audience. As the pop world became more sophisticated, the musicians themselves demanded better graphic presentation. By the mid-1960s, the pop world, through its association with talented artists and designers, was influencing the images of the graphic world. The work of the Push Pin Studios, with its strange and mysterious qualities, was adapted to serve the visual needs of the influential youth market.

The population boom encouraged consumerism in other fields. Thomas Cook, a long-established British travel firm, now beginning to be faced by a growing mass exodus to holiday beaches in Spain and Europe, transformed its traditional information pamphlet into a highly commercial production.

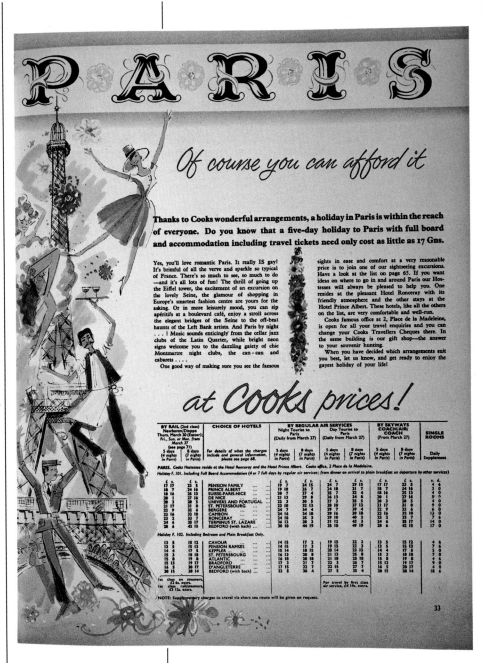

Thomas Cook brochure, Britain, 1961. The layout includes a lively continental style of illustration which contains the vital prices and travel information.

With the consumer boom came a need for more design talent to cope with the increased output of graphic information. This period marked the change in the structure of the old commercial art studios, and brought about a highly modern and sophisticated graphic design service industry, known today as design consultancies.

INFLUENCES

1. Full Fathom Five, *USA, c.1950. A late painting by Jackson Pollock. His action painting explored a new art concept of expressing feelings directly on to the canvas.*

2. *VW factory, Germany, 1938. The German achievement was to educate European designers in the manufacture of efficient and functional consumer goods.*

3. *Seymour Chwast, USA, c.1964. The early pioneering work of Push Pin Studios, a group of approximately 20 artists, explored new expressive art thinking and created some of the most daring and adventurous graphics of this period.*

4. *Lucky Strike pack, USA, c.1945. In the post-war years, the confidence of Americans in all they tackled and produced, greatly influenced the reshaping of Europe. This cigarette packet spells out this confidence.*

5

5. *Richard Hamilton, Britain, 1956. A collage produced from American magazine advert cuttings – the new society as seen by the artist.*

6. *Elvis Presley, USA, c.1955. Presley's influence, and his contemporaries', marked the beginning of a breakaway youth culture, challenging the beliefs and traditions of past generations.*

7

7. *USA, c.1950. Quite innocuous by today's standards, items such as these set the pace for consumerism when they first appeared.*

8. Fall *by Bridget Riley, Britain, 1963. Riley's work had a great influence on the evolution of graphic layout with her sensational, dazzling patterns.*

6

8

PHOTOGRAPHY

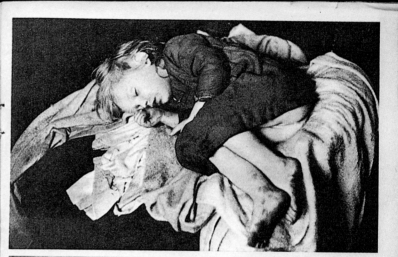

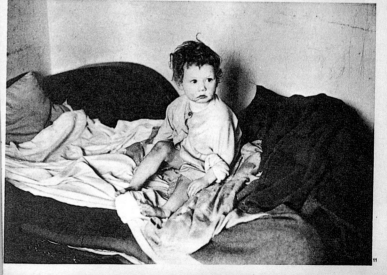

The Vs are prosperous; he owns a chain of shops, they live comfortably with four children whom they apparently love and care for well – and a fifth, the eldest, whom they hate. She was removed from home at a year old because of her mother's cruelty and cared for by grandparents. Recently, nearing school-leaving age, she returned to the Vs. Now when she comes home from school she is forced to do the housework, then remain in the scullery – where she eats her meals. She is forbidden to play with friends, is refused money to take extra sewing or cookery lessons; money given her by an aunt was confiscated by the parents. Anything she makes at school they burn. She has a habit of putting up an arm to defend herself from her mother's frequent clouts. She will probably have to be taken into the care of the local authority. She is intelligent, of good character. Why do the parents hate her?

is no time to stop and reflect upon strategy. Now, however, it is beginning to try to discover why these horrors happen; why a mother will leave her children for days without food, or a father cut a leather belt into thongs and harden it in the fire before beating his child until the flesh peels off.

Like the other welfare agencies, the N.S.P.C.C. will be helped in this task by the National Bureau for Co-operation in Child Care, an independent body set up recently under Dr Kellmer Pringle to co-ordinate information and gather evidence. But even classification, the first step to any scientific study, is not easy when the subject is cruelty to children.

There seems at first an easy division. There are neglect cases, where the difficulties of running a home overwhelm a mother who may be mentally defective, ill, or exhausted by too much child-bearing. There are the cruelties of stupid and violent parents – why expect a man who becomes aggressive after drinking to ignore the easy target of his own children? And there are the recognisably kinky, the perverts whose pleasure is to cause pain.

There are simple-minded mothers who bring to the task of rearing a family only the intelligence of a nine-year-old, and become overwhelmed as a nine-year-old would. Many cases of cruelty and neglect occur after a family has been rehoused. The extra strain of trying to keep up with the neighbours may prove too much for inadequate parents; a mess on the clean floor becomes an outrage where on a floor already encrusted with filth is was not.

Not every /continued on page 13

1. The Sunday Times, *Britain, 1965. The Sunday Times supplement was the first British magazine of its kind to offer a platform for young, talented photographers. Shown here are photographs by Anthony Armstrong-Jones (Snowdon), in an article in which serious editorial* comment is supported by documentary-style photography.

LIFE
INTERNATIONAL

HISTORIC DEFECTION OF RED AGENT REVEALS
SECRETS OF SECRET POLICE
'THOSE CALLAS SCANDALS'
BY MARIA CALLAS

MARILYN MONROE
IN NEWEST MOVIE

RECEIVED
1 5 MAY 1959
ANSD.............

MAY 25, 1959

REG. U.S. PAT. OFF.

2. Life International, *USA, 1959. Glamorous photography dominates the pages of this magazine, in which memorable images take precedence over copy.*

1 & 2 Miroir Sprint, France 1948. The cover photograph shows effective use of cropping, and the "O" of the title gives the illusion of being the football. The page layout, dominated by action photographs of track cyclists, is lively and full of movement. The text is limited, emphasizing the importance of the photographs, which convey the story with only the merest supporting text.

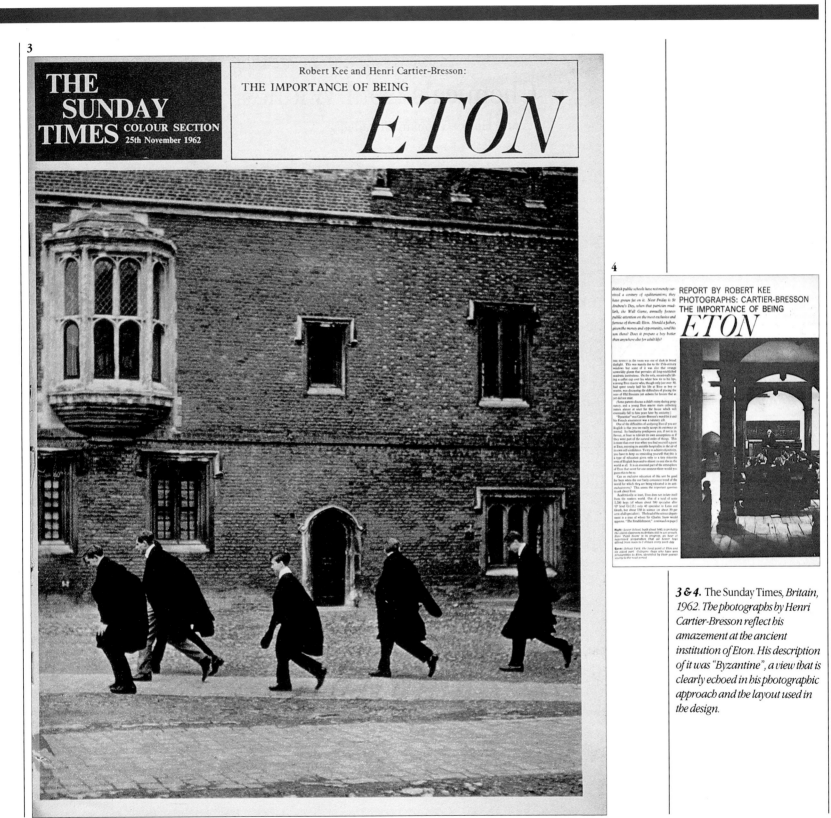

3 & 4. The Sunday Times, *Britain, 1962. The photographs by Henri Cartier-Bresson reflect his amazement at the ancient institution of Eton. His description of it was "Byzantine", a view that is clearly echoed in his photographic approach and the layout used in the design.*

Have something old?
Add something new

How to have a new room and keep some of the same old things

By Ethel Brostrom

Not all of us can redecorate our homes and start out with everything brand new. Most of us have to hang onto part of the old furnishings, sometimes for the sake of economy, sometimes because we like what we have. Then how can we make our room look new? How can an old piece or some other element be made part of a new scheme? In these rooms we show you three ways to go about redecorating around something you want to keep.

Below, you see how a room with "heirloom walls" can be skillfully redone so it looks new all over. At right is a pink and white room that demonstrates what to do when wall-to-wall carpeting is too good to replace. Below that, you see a room where a handsome old breakfront has been made the center of the new decorating scheme. One of these techniques may help with your problem rooms.

Fit the room around the rug

Suppose you want to redo your living room, but your carpeting is still good. Here we show you an example of how to work out a decorating scheme that includes the carpeting. The carpet is a rosy pink, and what we've done is to add a lot more of the same color. So pink and white striped wallpaper has been used on the walls. The woodwork and the ceiling are painted the same pink as the carpet. The whole room becomes pink and serves as a background for the furnishings—nubby-textured sofa, draperies and chair in a patterned fabric. Accent colors are pink and dark green.

New scheme but the same four walls

You'd redecorate often before you'd change beautiful paneled walls like these. How to get a new-looking room and keep the walls the same? If you have dark walls (as here) or very light walls, try our solution. Refurnish as though the walls weren't there, using other colors altogether. Here we've designed a brilliant and contrasting color scheme

around new carpeting and furniture. Bright oranges and yellows are harmonious with the brown wall. But the wall color itself is not repeated anywhere because it is to be played down. The vibrant green carpet and the scheme attract attention that the...

Drawings: Lillian Rawlings

Keep your antique

Want to redecorate the li...

At last—a home with room for everything

THE <u>RIGHT</u> WAY TO PAINT YOUR HOUSE
EASTER DINNER WITH LEG O' LAMB

Leg o' lamb
...easy and elegant!

By Helen W. Fritz

1, 2 & 3. Household, *USA, 1956. The consumer boom of the postwar years came to life in magazines of this kind, whose content encouraged a new mass-market affluence. The layouts and pictures use a simple, direct formula*
4. Ideal Home, *Britain, 1958. Advertising became a dominant feature of mass-market magazines.*

5. Household, *USA, 1953.*
Full-page pictures of food
followed by little text and smart
layout became the model for
future magazines.

6. Ideal Home, *Britain, 1959.*

7. Ideal Home, *Britain, 1958.*

8. Household, *USA, 1953.*

1. Daily Mirror, *Britain, 1945. First published in 1903, the newspaper broke new ground* by using bold, condensed headings with dramatic photographs.

Daily Mirror
VE-DAY!
IT'S OVER IN THE WEST

Tuesday, May 8, 1945 ONE PENNY
No. 12,911
Registered at G.P.O. as a Newspaper.

London had joy night

2. Daily Express, *Britain, 1953. Bold cross-heads are used to good effect within a traditional middle-market format.*

DAILY EXPRESS
STALIN IS DEAD
Moscow announcement at 1.7 a.m. today

3. Daily Mirror, *Britain, 1945. This dramatic double page spread depicts V-E day.*

LONDON TO BERLIN
A DIARY of the WAR
being an account of the victorious emergence of the British Empire and its Allies from the black waves of Fascism with which Germany and Italy engulfed Europe and threatened the world for six years

4. Wichita Beacon, *USA, 1950. The front page makes use of condensed items of news to round up current events.*

WICHITA BRIEFS
THE WICHITA BEACON EXTRA
'FIGHT TO THE DEATH' ORDER IS GIVEN GI'S IN SOUTH KOREA
Demand Block of Chinese Reds Into UN

5 & 6. Daily Mail, *Britain, 1953. The design and production were carefully considered for this most significant event, and the actual newspaper was reprinted in gold.*

7. Chicago Sun Times, *USA, 1962. The layout was made to reflect the importance of these dangerous and uncertain times, and illustration was used in an unprecedented way for the front page.*

8. Chicago Daily News, *USA, 1963. The world was shaken by this tragedy, and the layout artist was left with the minimum of copy to display on this page.*

9. The Washington Post, *USA, 1963. The end of an era was described in a formal format but, unusually, with a colour photograph.*

NEW STYLE MAGAZINES

1. Esquire, *USA, 1958. The layout design of this magazine was radically changed by the innovative ideas of Henry Wolf. This page demonstrates his concern for the unification of graphics and text.*

2. Viewpoint, *Britain, 1964. A short-lived magazine for a sophisticated youth culture, with layouts of great inventiveness. Note the two columns of text extracted from the article and integrated into the illustration.*

3. Life, *USA, 1964. The layout dramatizes the event photographically with subtle use of the graph to follow the event.*

4. Sunday Times Magazine, *Britain, 1962. This publication marked the beginning of a significant trend in newspaper magazines.*

Generations clash: they always have done; the jealousies on both sides are older than Lear. But now the clash reverberates round the world. The young have apparently lost the art of deference. On the pages to come the sides debate; and New Generationers discuss their life and times—their front is certainly divided.

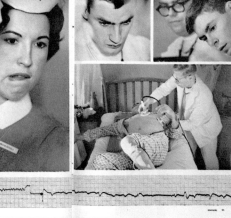

Toughest job: starting his heart

impresarios

Fielding on the boundary

Parnes, shillings and pence

5

Today it's no more daring to color your hair than to change your lipstick. For happy results, know what to do yourself and what to leave to experts

What you want to know about hair coloring

The changes you can make with temporary color are not drastic changes, but they can do wonderful things for your appearance. Temporary rinses, color sprays and color shampoos (which coat the hair with a transparent sheet of color) do a natural-looking job of brightening and adding high lights to "mousy" hair or of toning down too brassy locks. They can make hair that's starting to go gray newly flattering and can often be used to touch up permanently colored hair between salon visits.

When you want a complete color change from brown to blonde, from blonde to brunette, from gray to light brown, permanent coloring or bleaching is called for. Today's permanent or durable colorings are variously called tints, oil tints, color shampoos, color baths. Bleaches are often called "hair lighteners." How successful you will be at using these products yourself depends on your skill with your hair, your patience, your willingness to follow directions to the letter. If you're planning a radical change, it's best to entrust permanent coloring—certainly the first time—to a trained beautician who understands exactly how texture, porosity and general condition of the hair will affect results. Unlike temporary colorings, permanent tints penetrate the hair shaft and actually deposit pigments in somewhat the same way as natural color. Bleaches take away natural color rapidly or gradually, depending on how strong they are and how long they are left on.

To find the color that is right for you, remember:
• Color cards at cosmetic counters show the shades as they would turn out on absolutely *white* hair.
• To intensify natural color, choose a *temporary* color one to two shades *deeper* than your own hair tone; use copper, bronze or auburn shades to add red high lights, gold shades for golden high lights, and ash blonde, platinum or steel gray shades to tone down brassy hair.
• To get the effect you want with *permanent* tints, choose a color that looks two shades *lighter* on the color card.
• You can make the most of gray hair with temporary rinses—light platinum or pearly to add sparkle and tone down yellow streaks without adding color, darker to add soft, smoky overtones—or you can disguise it with a permanent color. If you tint, don't try to duplicate your original shade. Complexion tones change with the years and lighter, softer hair tones are usually more flattering.
• Remember that bleaching is a progressive process. To go from very dark to platinum blonde, for instance, hair

goes through successive stages of brown, red and gold. The "gradual lighteners" (applications can be repeated up to six times) are a safe and simple do-it-yourself way for natural blondes or brownettes to avoid a "faded" look.
• Remember too that not everyone has the complexion to become a successful blonde. If your skin is olive-toned or sallow, don't try to be a silver blonde. You'll need a tint with warmer tones — such as auburn or warm brown.

Must you be a slave to colored hair? Depends on what you consider "slavery." If you take for granted a weekly shampoo and set, a weekly manicure, a permanent at regular intervals, you won't be alarmed by the grooming needs of tinted hair. Temporary colorings ordinarily take only a few minutes to apply, but most must be repeated with each shampoo. A permanent tint may add as much as an hour to the shampooing process and may need to be touched up at the roots every three to five weeks. Bleaching can take up to two hours per application; a brunette may need to be retouched at the roots in ten days to two weeks.

Do you care for colored hair differently? General care is the same, but it should be a little more tender. Faithful brushing with a not-too-stiff brush, regular shampooing with a mild shampoo are recommended. Don't overuse hair sprays—too many coatings may dull colored hair. Do protect colored hair from sun and salt water. Both can cause streaking or fading.

If you give yourself a permanent, choose one that is gentle strength, with a separate neutralizer, and be sure to take a test curl and follow directions *exactly*. The reason: Coloring hair makes it more porous and this causes a permanent to take faster. If a test curl seems frizzy, discontinue the permanent until conditioning treatments have made it look and feel more natural. Never try to tint and permanent simultaneously. For best results, have your permanent a week or more before you plan to color.

Will coloring hurt your hair? Properly used, no. In fact, women with fine, flyaway hair often find that permanent coloring after a time gives their hair more body. This is because using permanent tints and bleaches eventually causes the hair shaft to swell. Coarse hair, on the other hand, may need regular cream rinses to keep it smooth and silky. Frizzy, hard-to-manage hair may be improved in texture by temporary color rinses in cream-base solution, which helps tame it. *(Continued on page 74)*

72 McCall's, October 1958

McCall's, October 1958 73

6

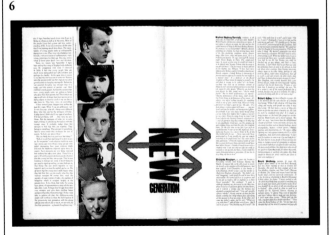

7

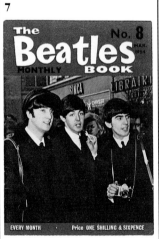

5. McCall's, *USA, 1958. The layout brings together manipulated photography, illustrative colour and crisp, excellently proportioned typography. The two pages are linked with the coloured discs to give a light, refreshing feel. Art Director Otto Starch, photographer John Stewar.*

6. Viewpoint, *Britain, 1964. Excellent use of the graphic device and white space to link the outer columns of copy.*

7. The Beatles Monthly Book, *Britain, 1964. Youth culture was generating its own publications, although, in the early days, these lacked expertise and sophistication.*

NEW STYLE MAGAZINES

1, 2 & 3. Typographica, *Britain,* 1962. The first of these spreads shows a well-organized use of a modern layout in which the photographic, diagrammatic and text images link to the wide, single-column format. The second shows the single-column format, with the wide gutter used for captions. The final spread exploits space to complement the illustrative matter on display.

4. Typographica, *Britain,* 1962. The magazine's rather formal layout is cunningly interrupted by the carefully crafted pages of prints that can be pulled out from the central spine.

a Pelican Book 6'-

Archaic Egypt

W. B. Emery

e Vedel

a Pelican Book

The Affluent Society

J. K. Galbraith

Larry Carter

4

NEW AMERICAN DESIGN

personal answer—: but how should they, who have already flung themselves together and no longer mark off and distinguish themselves from each other, who therefore no longer possess anything of their own selves, be able to find a way out of themselves, out of the depth of their already shattered solitude?

They act out of common helplessness, and then, if, with the best intentions, they try to avoid the convention that occurs to them (say, marriage), they land in the tentacles of some less loud, but equally deadly conventional solution; for then everything far around them is—convention; where people act out of a prematurely fused, turbid communion, *every* move is convention: every relation to which such entanglement leads has its convention, be it ever so unusual (that is, in the ordinary sense immoral); why, even separation would here be a conventional step, an impersonal chance decision without strength and without fruit.

Whoever looks seriously at it finds that neither for death, which is difficult, nor for difficult love has any explanation, any solution, any hint or way yet been discerned; and for these two problems that we carry wrapped up and hand on without opening, it will not be possible to discover any general rule resting in agreement. But in the same measure in which we begin as individuals to put life to the test, we shall, being individuals, meet these things at closer range. The demands which the difficult work of love makes upon our development are more than life-size, and as beginners we are not up to them. But if we nevertheless hold out and take this love upon us as burden and apprenticeship, instead of losing ourselves in all the light and frivolous play, behind which people have hidden from the most earnest earnestness of their existence—then a little progress and an alleviation will perhaps be perceptible to those who come long after us; that would be much.

Progressive democracy and love

Progressive democracy, I believe, has to be based on and sustained by progressive love because love, too, has to feel itself as new, as an eternal present. So democracy as it moves onward will be ever new because its love is and will be ever new. I think of life as an eternal material and spiritual newness produced by continual love, everyday love, love which rises every day like the dawn. The complete man must be new, a child each day in all of this activities, major and minor (work, rest, sleep) if he wants them all to have this necessary quality by virtue of which he can leave them with pleasure and return to take them up again with pleasure. The awakening of a human being in despondency or joy ought to be a call to arms, a call to understand life in its entirety each day, our own life and that of others. I imagine all of humanity getting up each morning as an introduction to my daily life, taking from all of this what I should, and how useful to me is this exemplary preoccupation! To understand the daily lives of others and to share them with a tranquil, cultivated instinct, with a sympathy for what is constructive and what is uncon-

Paul Davis

HOLIDAY ISSUE OF THE *Push Pin Graphic.* NUMBER THIRTY-NINE

3

Thomas, a hard-working businessman. They were married and went to live with the Thomas family on a street and in a house that was little different from what she had always known. How could she escape from her drab surroundings into the brighter life she knew existed somewhere? That was the question that insistently gnawed at her. After two years of marriage she left Thomas and returned to her mother's home, despondent but determined and fiercely hungry. She was now eighteen, with an ethereal beauty, and she was not going to waste that beauty in a town where even the clothes hung out on the line where even the gray with smoke, the color of the gloom that surrounded her. With another girl she went to work in Pittsburgh as a model in a fashion show in Kaufman's department store. The show lasted only a week but Olive had her taste of glamor, the feel of silk against her young body, and having had it she wanted more and more.

On borrowed money she came to New York during the winter of 1913 and supported herself by posing for photographers and artists until she managed to get in to see Ziegfeld several months later. Almost from the moment she stepped on the stage Olive was quickly acknowledged by the front-row connoisseurs as breathtaking. When she left the stage to go to Hollywood she was making $2,500 a week and, if for no other reason than to watch her parade as a

4

5

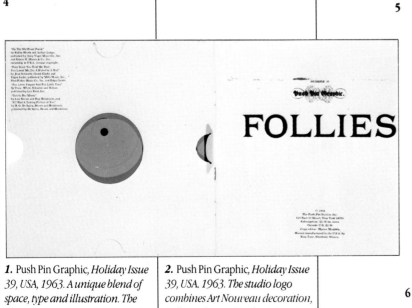

FOLLIES

1. Push Pin Graphic, *Holiday Issue 39, USA, 1963. A unique blend of space, type and illustration. The single inner column is linked to the outer margin by the minuscule heading. Drawing by Paul Davis.*

2. Push Pin Graphic, *Holiday Issue 39, USA, 1963. The studio logo combines Art Nouveau decoration, calligraphic and Gothic letters, in an original blend of distinctive styling.*

3. Push Pin Graphic 45, *USA, 1964. The format was in continuous flux, although the distinctive blend of type and illustration continued. Pages by Milton Glaser.*

4. Push Pin Graphic 45, *USA, 1964. Title page with interlocking plastic record.*

5. Push Pin Graphic 45, *USA, 1964. Record which forms an integral part of the design.*

6. Push Pin Graphic 45, *USA, 1964. Front cover engineered to carry the plastic disc.*

6

NEW AMERICAN DESIGN

1, 2 & 3. Push Pin Graphic 44, *USA,*
1964. Cover design, title page and
one spread.

1

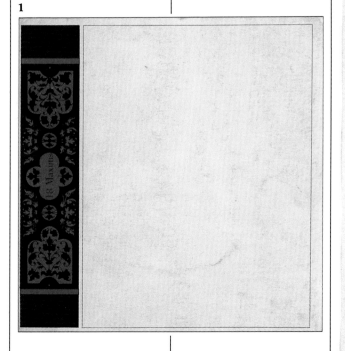

2

3

4

It is through Art, and through Art only,
that we can realize our perfection;
through Art and Art only
that we can shield ourselves
from the sordid perils of actual existence.

4

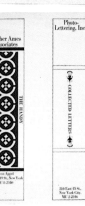

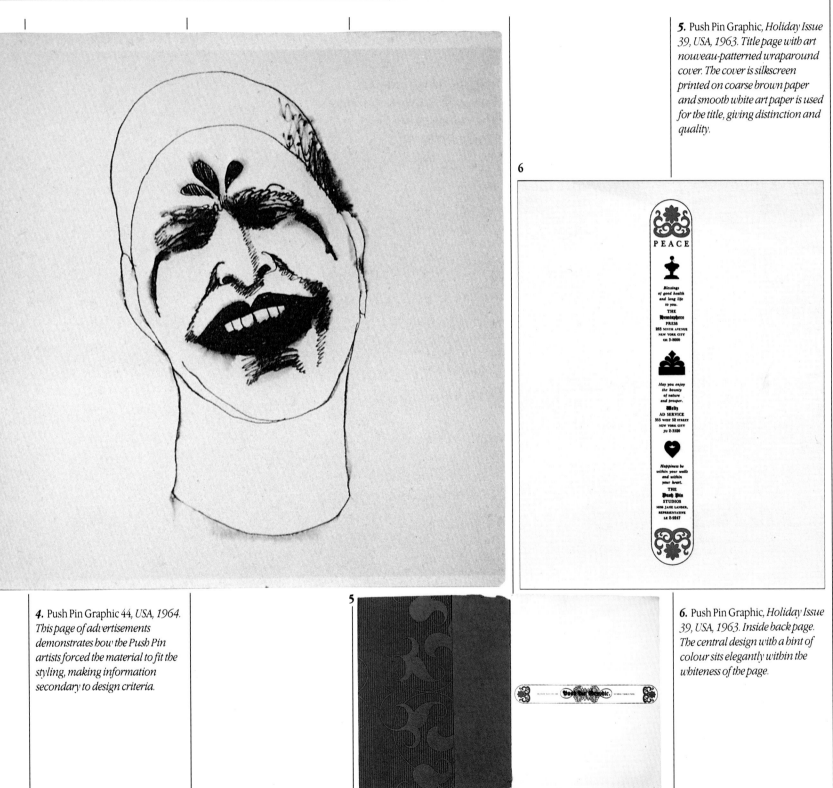

5. Push Pin Graphic, *Holiday Issue 39, USA, 1963.* Title page with art nouveau-patterned wraparound cover. The cover is silkscreen printed on coarse brown paper and smooth white art paper is used for the title, giving distinction and quality.

4. Push Pin Graphic 44, *USA, 1964.* This page of advertisements demonstrates how the Push Pin artists forced the material to fit the styling, making information secondary to design criteria.

6. Push Pin Graphic, *Holiday Issue 39, USA, 1963.* Inside back page. The central design with a hint of colour sits elegantly within the whiteness of the page.

NEW LAYOUT DESIGN

1. Pagina, *Italy, 1962. The layouts of* Pagina *are themselves unique and led design at this time.*
2 & 3. Neue Graphik, *Switzerland, 1959-60. At this time Swiss design was changing the face of layout in Europe.*
4. Neue Graphik, *Switzerland, 1959. Laying out the inside pages required precision and skill to accommodate the tri-lingual copy.*

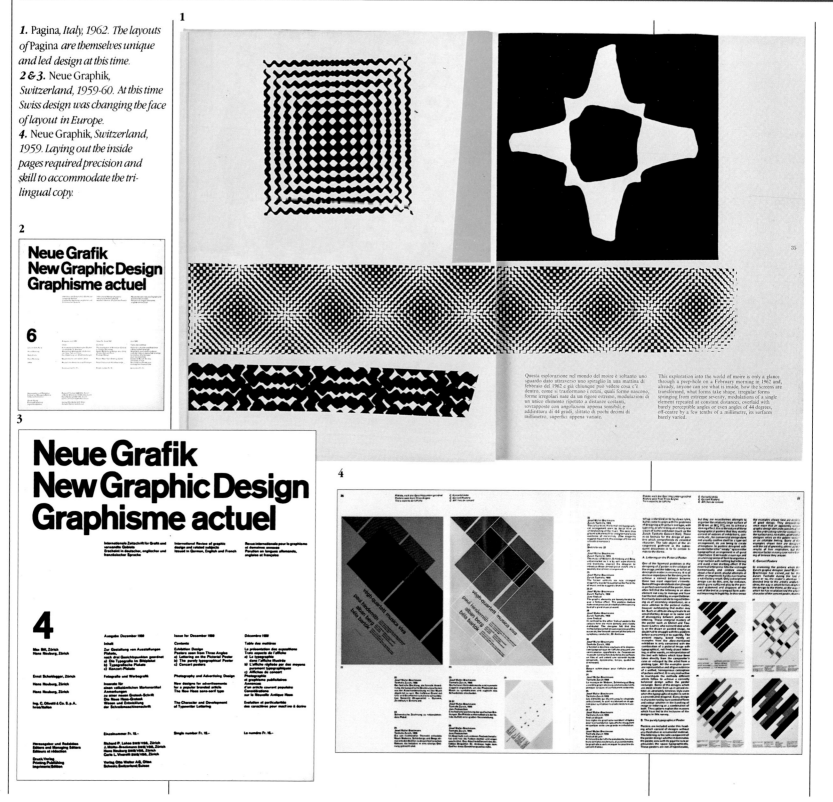

Questa esplorazione nel mondo del moiré è soltanto uno sguardo dato attraverso uno spiraglio in una mattina di febbraio del 1962 e già chiunque può vedere cosa c'è dentro, come si trasformano i retini, quali forme nascono, forme irregolari nate da un rigore estremo, modulazioni di un unico elemento ripetuto a distanze costanti, sovrapposte con angolazioni appena sensibili, e addirittura di 44 gradi, slittato di pochi decimi di millimetro, superfici appena variate.

This exploration into the world of moiré is only a glance through a peep-hole on a February morning in 1962 and, already, anyone can see what is inside, how the screens are transformed, what forms take shape, irregular forms springing from extreme severity, modulations of a single element repeated at constant distances, overlaid with barely perceptible angles or even angles of 44 degrees, off-centre by a few tenths of a millimetre, its surfaces barely varied.

5. Print, *USA, 1963. The front cover of America's graphic design magazine was designed by S. Neil Fujita and set by Franklin typographers.*
6 & 7. Print, *USA, 1962-3. The publication is a rich blend of new graphics mixed with the crafts of the old commercial art practice.*

THEATER

1, 2 & 3. Châtelet, *France*, c.1945. The layouts incorporate photography and line illustrations in a style that echoes both the period and the nature of the theatrical production.

4. Oklahoma, *Britain*, c.1950. Comparing the layout of this handbill with the more formal earlier programme shows how the design expresses the spirit of the production for a modern theatre-going public.

5. Oklahoma, *Britain*, 1947. This programme cover reflects the formality of the theatre's image at the time of the first night of this show, which became a landmark in new theatre productions.

Oklahoma!

Theatre Royal Drury Lane

Charles the Second

This design is copied from the original Charter granted by King Charles II to Thomas Killigrew in 1663 the original document is still in existence.

5

6

NEW THEATRE
ST. MARTIN'S LANE, W.C.2

Licensed by the Lord Chamberlain to SIR BRONSON ALBERY
Lessees: THE WYNDHAM THEATRES LTD.
Managing Directors: SIR BRONSON ALBERY and DONALD ALBERY

oliver!

A new musical
book, music and lyrics by
LIONEL BART

1/-

7

THE
ORIGINAL
NEW
THEATRE
CAST
RECORDING OF

oliver!

by LIONEL BART

O SKL 4105 O LK 4359

DECCA

The Decca Record Company Ltd
Decca House
Albert Embankment
London S E 1

OLIVER!

Book, Music and Lyrics by LIONEL BART

Oliver Twist	KEITH HAMSHERE

At the Workhouse

Mr. Bumble, *the Beadle*	PAUL WHITSUN-JONES
Mrs. Corney, *the Matron*	HOPE JACKMAN
Old Sally, *a pauper*	BETTY TURNER

At the Undertaker's

Mr. Sowerberry, *the Undertaker*	BARRY HUMPHRIES
Mrs. Sowerberry, *his wife*	SONIA FRASER
Charlotte, *their daughter*	APPLE BROOK
Noah Claypole, *their apprentice*	TREVOR RAY

At the Thieves' Kitchen

Fagin	RON MOODY
The Artful Dodger	MARTIN HORSEY
Nancy	GEORGIA BROWN
Bet	CARLA CHALLENOR
Bill Sikes	DANNY SEWELL

At the Brownlow's

Mr. Brownlow	GEORGE BISHOP
Mr. Grimwig	CLAUDE JONES
Mrs. Bedwin	ELSIE WINSOR

Workhouse Boys and Fagin's Gang:

FRANCIS ATTARD, KEITH COLLINS, PETER EVELEIGH, CLIVE GREEN, PETER HAYES, LAURIE HEATH, DEREK HUGHES, ALAN JONES, JONATHAN MORRIS, PAUL NORMAN, MICHAEL PHILLIPS, BILLY PRESTON, BRUCE PROCHNIK, ALAN RIDGWAY.

Londoners:

SALLY BITTON, ANNA LEROY, JEAN ANN PAGE, JANET PATE, ELIZABETH PERRY, JULIA SUTTON, DAVID BEAUMONT, JONATHAN BROMLEY, ERIC HOLMES, BOB INGLIS, ROBERT KEMP, LARRY OAKS, ROSS PIERSON, STANLEY PRICE, BRIAN SCOTT.

6 & 7. Oliver, *Britain, 1960.
This charming combination of
illustration and type is a
refreshing, smart approach to
layout design.*

BOOKS

1, 2 & 3. The Practice of Design, *Britain, 1946. Design and layout by Hans Schleger. The outer cover is bound in a traditional manner, while the inside pages use the flexible system of spiral binding and the layout breaks all the traditional rules by displaying sub-headings in the scholars' margin and main headings at the foot of the page.*
4. Les Contes Drolatiques, *Britain, 1945. Design and layout by Hans Schleger.*

1

2

3

4

5 & 6. Plaisir de France, *France, 1946. This journal, in bound book form, reflects the parallel development in France of the consumer boom.*

7 & 8. Time, *Britain, 1960. Breaking the tradition of book design, the horizontal format allows the elongated shapes to be exploited in the layout of pictures and text.*

BROCHURES

1 & 2. *Austin Motor Company Limited, Britain, 1957. A very large-format brochure, with an almost A3 page size, makes use of background colour and reversed-out illustration, overlaid with heavily retouched photographs.*

3. *Chrysler Corporation, Dodge Division, USA, 1959. The large landscape format, supported by classic style illustrations, uses a wide three-column grid.*

SOUND CONSTRUCTION

A105 DE LUXE SALOON

Super performance and unostentatious luxury being the keynote of this magnificent saloon, and every conceivable accessory for the comfort of its driver and passengers has been included in its specification.   It is to-day's greatest thrill in motoring—it's new, it's exciting to drive !

AUSTIN
A·95 WESTMINSTER AND A·105 DE-LUXE SALOONS

Coronet Series

Your Low-Cost Invitation to Luxury Motoring!

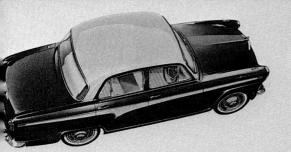

ATTENTION TO DETAIL ...

Beautifully styled, stainless steel discs cover the entire wheels of the A105. They are easy to keep clean, and blending with the white-side-wall tyres, add considerably to the grace and dignity of the car.

The new Austin A105 De Luxe Saloon is available in a wide range of modern and appealing colours, both the interior trim and exterior paintwork being in full dual-tone finish. A vast amount of luggage slides easily into place on the low-loading platform of the luggage compartment and such items as starting handle and jack are clipped unobtrusively to the sides.
Every part of the A105, from its hooded headlamps to the sleek rear end presents a pleasant, evenly balanced appearance—a car suitable for any occasion, well able to take its place as an Ambassador of British engineering at its best.

Twin fog lamps provide a brilliant flood of light at low level in front of the car, unaccompanied by back-glare. The car can thus be kept moving with greatly reduced driving strain.

A windscreen washer is neatly installed beneath the bonnet of the Austin A105. With no more inconvenience than merely pressing a button on the fascia, a mud-splashed screen can be automatically washed by twin jets.

YOU CAN DEPEND ON IT

4 & 5. *Ford Motor Company Ltd, Britain, c.1960. The front cover depicts a new stylish use of fast-moving photography, with the text exploiting the shapes and colours within the photograph. The centre spread echoes the mood and tells a story visually.*

4

ZEPHYR 6

5

BROCHURES

1, 2 & 3, *R.M.S.* Queen Elizabeth, *Britain, 1949. Superb elegance and an uncluttered, regal appearance combine in this brochure, which communicates the grandeur of the Cunard liner.*

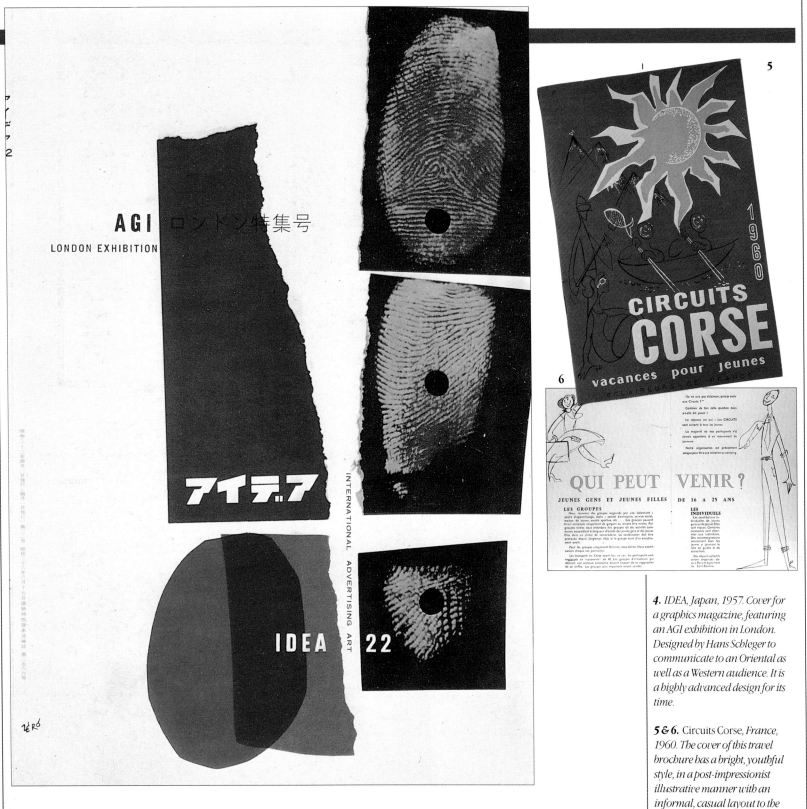

4. IDEA, Japan, 1957. Cover for a graphics magazine, featuring an AGI exhibition in London. Designed by Hans Schleger to communicate to an Oriental as well as a Western audience. It is a highly advanced design for its time.

5 & 6. Circuits Corse, France, 1960. The cover of this travel brochure has a bright, youthful style, in a post-impressionist illustrative manner with an informal, casual layout to the inside spread.

BROCHURES

Forestal Quebracho

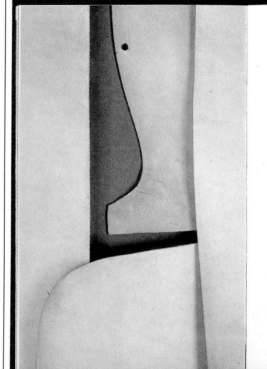

Schnellgerbung

Viele Schnellgerbmethoden ergeben eine beträchtliche Menge Gerbbrühe, die nur eine mittelmässige Stärke besitzt. Sie bleibt nach der Gerbung in Überschuss aus und in anderen Abteilungen der Gerberei verwendet werden. Dieses spielt keine Rolle, wo die Häute vor der Gerbung kroupeniert werden, weil die Schnellgerbung der Kroupons angeführt und die überflüssige Gerbbrühe bei einer herkömmlichen Gerbung der Garnitur verwendet werden kann. Wo jedoch die Gerbung von ganzen oder halben Häuten angeführt wird, ist es notwendig, eine Methode anzuwenden, bei welcher alle vorhandenen Gerbstoffe innerhalb des Gerbsystems verbracht werden, sodass keine Reste anderweitig eingesetzt werden müssen. Diese Schwierigkeit kann man überwinden, wenn die Gerbung in einem Fass mit Hilfe von konzentrierter Brühe oder pulverisiertem Quebracho-Extrakt ausgeführt wird. Da jedoch durch dieses Verfahren ein gezogener Narben entstehen kann, muss gewöhnlich eine Vorgerbung vor der Fassgerbung mit Quebracho-Extrakt erfolgen. Eine Schnellgerbmethode, die auf diesem Prinzip aufgebaut ist, wird unter der Überschrift 'Gerbung x1' beschrieben.

Das Problem der überschüssigen Brühe kann man auch lösen, wenn die anfängliche Gerbung in einer Grube mit starker Brühe durchgeführt wird und danach die Gerbung in einem Fass mit Hilfe von einer gewissen Menge Brühe aus der Grube beendet wird, die entweder mit konzentriertem flüssigem, festem oder pulverisiertem Extrakt verstärkt wurde. Dieses System, welches unter 'Gerbung x2a' beschrieben ist, arbeitet sehr gut, vorausgesetzt, dass gewisse Vorsichtsmassnahmen getroffen werden, die gewährleisten, dass die Brühe im Fass in gutem Zustand gehalten wird.

Manchmal zieht man es vor, eine Schnellgerbung in Gruben auszuführen, wobei die von den Gruben abgezogene starke Brühe in anderen Abteilungen der Gerberei eingesetzt werden kann. Für solche Bedingungen wird die Gerbung x2 unten beschrieben.

Ganz gleich, welche Schnellgerbmethode angewendet wird, wichtig ist immer, dass man vor der Gerbung eine wirksame Entkälkung vornimmt. Vorschläge für solche Entkälkungsmethoden folgen.

49

WINTER SUNSHINE

RIVIERA HOLIDAYS

MARKETING INFORMATION PLEASE DO NOT REMOVE

3 & 4. Riviera brochure, Britain, 1963. This early design gives a cheerful feeling.

5 & 6. Thomas Cook, Britain, 1961. The magazine-style page design and layout pre-date the commercialism of the present.

3

4

1 & 2. Forestal Quebracho booklet, Britain, 1962. Designed by Hans Schleger. An example of imaginative photographic art direction, using the natural art forms created by leather to complement the white page and tonal panel of text.

15 DAY HOLIDAY BY SCHEDULED AIR SERVICE

Rightly called "Pearl of the Mediterranean" MAJORCA is one of the loveliest places in which to spend a winter holiday, offers warmth, beauty, romance, magnificent scenery, sun-swept beaches, ancient folk-lore, gardens filled with tropical plants, and many, many more attractions.

PALMA, our winter holiday centre will enchant you. It's intriguing shops, its hospitable people, all play their part in making a holiday that will long live in your memory.

HOTEL VERSALLES. Superior hotel, overlooking Palma Bay. All rooms are spacious and with hot and cold water supply. Splendid service and cuisine.

HOTEL ZAIDA. First class, overlooks PALMA BAY. All rooms are spacious with bath. Excellent cuisine.

HOTEL COSTA AZUL. Superior, on main sea promenade. Excellent food and service. All rooms with bath.

HOTEL ALCINA. First class. Renowned cuisine and service. on main promenade. All rooms with bath. Beautiful garden for sunbathing.

HOTEL DUX. Typical Spanish superior first class hotel on main promenade. Superb food. Spacious rooms with bath.

MAJORCA—and the Sun drenched Balearics

HOTEL SARATOGA. Newly built first class hotel in town centre. All rooms with bath and terrace. Luxurious service and excellent food. Own swimming pool.

HOTEL ALMUDIANA. Modern hotel in centre of PALMA, 70 bedrooms with every comfort. Superb views. All rooms with bath or shower. Spanish and International cuisine. Dancing daily.

HOTEL BAHIA PALACE. Famous de-luxe hotel overlooking the bay. All rooms have own bath. Own swimming pool, night club, superb cuisine, splendid services. Spanish and International cuisine.

GRAN HOTEL MEDITERRANEO. Foremost of the de-luxe hotels. Situated on the main promenade. All rooms with private bath and terrace. Typical Spanish atmosphere, gay, friendly, hospitable. Four bars. Night club. Own swimming pool. Superb cuisine.

PRICES 15 DAY HOLIDAY BY SCHEDULED AIR SERVICES
By air (Tourist Day flights) to Palma. Departures in accordance with Air Companies' Schedules

HOTEL	Holiday Number RM 1	15 day holiday (14 nights hotel)
Versailles	54	19 0
*Zaida	62	2 0
*Costa Azul	62	18 0
Alcina	63	6 0
Dux	63	10 0
Saratoga	63	16 0
Almudiana	68	18 0
*Bahia Palace	77	14 0
*Gran Mediterraneo	81	15 0

* At hotels marked with asterisk there are additional daily charges for the period 22 December to 6th January.

Air travel from the provinces can be arranged at the additional charge: from Birmingham £1.16.0; from Manchester £2.12.0; from Belfast, Edinburgh or Glasgow, £5.5.0.

All hotels shown are available from November 1st to March 31st 1963 with departures as operated by National Airlines according to Company Schedules.

THE PRICE INCLUDES

Tourist Day Flights to Palma and return; transfers in Majorca; 14 nights hotel accommodation with full board; Spanish Airport Tax; services of Miss Toni Ressmann, our resident representative. Holidays may be extended to comply with your wishes, up to 23 days.

San Remo

"it's gay, it's exciting, it's colourful, it's marvellous"

You'll have the time of your life in San Remo! It's the gayest, most brilliant resort on the Italian Riviera—the largest too! You'll love the fine sandy beach dotted with bright umbrellas, love too the Corso Imperatrice: the broad, colourful promenade lined with gardens, palm trees and flowers. The wide avenues and elegant shops of the modern town make the ideal setting for your holiday. But don't miss the fun of exploring the picturesque mediaeval quarter or visiting some of the colourful little villages nearby. Turn to the list of sightseeing excursions on page 65. Just look at all there is to do: gorgeous swimming, boating and water-ski-ing and so much else besides. And what a wonderful night life! Lively cafés for dancing, cabarets and all the excitement of the Casino.

One of our Hostesses in San Remo stays at the first-grade Grand Hotel des Anglais, standing on elevated ground in its own magnificent gardens. In the most fashionable part of San Remo near the sea, it has wonderfully comfortable rooms, a lift, bar, and excellent food and service. Our other Hostess stays at the Astoria West End, also first-grade. Near the beach, this good hotel has an easy-going, friendly atmosphere. Another place to stay is the Villa Mio Riposo, a pleasant hotel reached by a series of a hundred steps.

Plan your holiday through Cooks and have a glorious sunny holiday completely free from care.

from £24.10s.

The sunny terrace of the Grand Hotel des Anglais.

Our Hostesses in front of the Hotel Astoria West End.

holidaymaking

COOKS
DEAN & DAWSON

Book at any branch of COOKS, DEAN & DAWSON, PICKFORDS or any appointed agent.

7. Skytours, Britain, 1964. Strong primary colours are used visually to separate the layout and to give the impression of sky and sand.

1964/5 WINTER HOLIDAYS

SkyTours

BRITANNIA AIRWAYS
DAY FLIGHTS TO
MAJORCA   CANARY
(PALMA)   ISLANDS
                              (TENERIFE)

15 DAYS
INCLUSIVE FROM **47** GNS.

15 DAYS
INCLUSIVE FROM **74** GNS

DEPART 11 A.M. FORTNIGHTLY ON SATURDAYS COMMENCING DECEMBER 8TH
LAST DEPARTURE APRIL 12TH

FORTNIGHTLY ON SUNDAYS AT 9.30 A.M. COMMENCING DECEMBER 8TH
LAST DEPARTURE APRIL 11TH

Oz, Britain, 1967. Art directed by Martin Sharp.

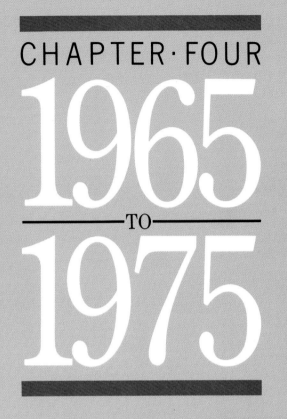

CHAPTER·FOUR

1965 TO 1975

INTRODUCTION

By 1965 babies born in the "baby boom" of the post-war years had grown into a highly influential generation, and the demands of youth consumerism provided an opportunity for creative companies to break the mould of traditional visual ideas. For the first time, young people were presented with images that directly related to their philosophy and aspirations. Nervousness about the intransigence of adult control and the political establishment was emphasized by young people's colourful and striking psychedelic imagery, and their ideals were beginning to rock the establishment in both Europe and America.

Throughout the world, new and exciting plans were evolving from the activities and discussions of this young generation, and the main stimulus for this identifiably different cultural standpoint was generated through its music. The physical music of the 1950s was giving way to more refined sounds: the protest songs of Bob Dylan, Joan Baez and Pete Seger; the raw influence of Southern American black music; and the working-class protest songs of the pop musicians. By the late 1960s, the pop culture, with its voracious appetite for the new, embraced promiscuity, hippies, drugs and the exploration of Eastern mysticism and ancient religions. From this mixture of Oriental culture, with its rich visual heritage, there resulted the explosion of psychedelic art, and its influence on clothing and fashion in general.

Magazines as the Voice of Youth

Magazines evolved as the voice of this new population. *Twen*, with its innovative design by Willy Fleckhaus, promoted the pop culture with stunning black pages with reversed-out text and dynamic, "arty" photography. The influence of this German magazine was felt by designers throughout the world. *Twen* represented the logical development of layout design, but at the same time magazines such as *Oz*, edited by Richard Neville and art directed by Martin Sharp, showed an alternative visual approach to layout design. Born out of the need for a magazine geared to the growing hippie culture, *Oz* explored the new wave of visual ideas.

By the 1960s the standardized instant letter forms were being produced by Letraset and phototypesetting and traditional hot metal typesetting offered opportunities to designers to simplify their processes. Under these circumstances the presentation of hippie imagery can be likened to the stubborn refusal of William Morris to accept the new technology of his age. Art school graduates perceived the use of rub-down lettering as an artless, functional activity that was out of tune with their own creative aspirations. It was difficult, in those early days, to comprehend where the traditional art processes and the new business-like graphic design practices interlocked.

Nova represents the philosophy and ideas of the 1960s. A well-structured, well-designed glossy magazine, it was

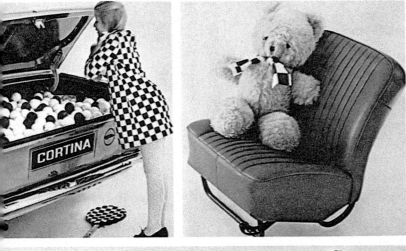

More Space. More Comfort!

New Cortina gives you more room to stretch —in every direction!

The bucket seats in front are deep, soft, relaxing with firm lateral support to keep you gently in your place.

The rear seat is equally comfortable with more hip room and shoulder room than you ever dreamed was possible within a car of Cortina's compact exterior dimension. This extra space, like Cortina's ample leg room, is achieved by brilliant design engineering making ingenious use of curved doors and side windows.

Cortina has plenty of boot space too. Its 21 cu. ft. copes easily with the week's groceries, or the family's luggage for a two week holiday.

"The overriders shown on this Cortina De Luxe are FoMoCo accessories, available at extra cost."

Ford Cortina brochure, Britain, c.1967. In the late 1960s London led the world in fashion and design, as is shown by the unusual flamboyance of this layout and the fashions illustrated.

The Butterfly Ball and the Grasshopper's Feast, *Britain, 1973. The astonishing skills of Alan Aldridge came together in this masterpiece of layout and illustration.*

INTRODUCTION

art directed by such leading practitioners as Harry Peccinotti and David Hillman, and its reputation as a platform for aspiring talent from the 1960s gave the underground art forms a place at the cutting edge of popular imagery. Designers such as Alan Aldridge, known for his colourful airbrush and line illustrations, set the style for this period. *Nova*'s daring articles swept away the publishing taboos of the past with explicit articles and provocative photography. Its layout, influenced to a degree by *Twen*, made use of bold type and reversed-out pages.

Design Consultancies and the Graphic Design Industry

The early 1960s had seen a boom in photography, but now it seemed that distinctive illustration and photography could coexist. The formation of business-like design consultancies was resulting in some outstanding success stories. The role of these consultancies, as design advisers in the creation of new product and service areas, gave graphic designers prestige and status. No longer would designers be confused with the commercial artists of the past, as a pride and professionalism in their approach generated a new confidence in the industry.

In the past, the distinctions between the work produced in the advertising agency studios and that produced in the commercial design studios, were unclear. Advertising agencies, which naturally controlled press and TV promotions, often found themselves co-ordinating the promotional material, such as brochures and even packaging design, so that design studios had to rely on the crumbs left by the advertising agencies. Now was the time that graphic designers realized that they could offer something that could not be provided by advertising agencies.

Their knowledge of the graphic elements, such as typography and the techniques involved in the manipulation of images, allowed graphic designers to make an impressive contribution to sales of consumer products, and to the way these were presented. There was no turning back for this new, aspiring industry. Companies were formed to specialize in the various divisions of graphic design, and designers such as F. H. K. Henrion and Hans Schleger led the trend towards concepts of corporate identity, replacing the traditional, but rather underdeveloped, company logo.

This concept was not confined simply to logo design, however. It affected every piece of graphic design information. From the specialist images required by banks, publishing houses and the like, to holiday brochures, the product and its layout and design had to reflect the audience it was designed for. "Inexpensive"

no longer meant "badly-put-together" publicity. The designer's task was to extract the best from the product he served and to reshape it into an appropriate package to communicate to an identifiable audience. Designers kept in touch with international developments in their industry through the publications that featured the best designs of the period. It was now possible, by studying *Graphis*, *Modern Publicity* or the *Design and Art Director's Annuals*, specifically to identify popular trends and the designers responsible for them.

Awards, too, became highly sought after as a way of attracting new clients and enhancing the quality of work in which the studio was involved.

Sgt. Pepper's Lonely Hearts Club Band, EMI Records, Britain, 1967. Although this is a studio layout (where the major part of this work has been captured in one photograph) additions were made to the final print. The importance of this piece is that it carries a major cast of 1960s' icons and personalities.

Design and Fine Art

With their broad vision of the visual world, designers continued to look towards the world of fine art as a source of reference and as a means of creative inspiration.

Experimentation by American and European Pop artists and their close links with graphic imagery acted as an incentive to individual designers. Both Roy Lichtenstein's approach to comic' strip art and David Hockney's individual approach played their part in shaping graphic design. Artists like Peter Blake were also involved in graphic design, as his work for the "Sgt Pepper's Lonely Hearts Club Band" album was clearly to prove. The imagery of Andy Warhol extended far beyond his influential paintings and into the public eye. His own image was incorporated into graphic layouts, and

Twen, Germany, 1969. This leader in youth magazine design with its reversed-out text and artfully cropped pictures, was a creative source for many subsequent titles such as Nova.

presented on the pages of magazines such as *Eye*, along with that of others seeking to be part of the pop world.

By the mid-1970s the failure of *Nova*, the *Oz* trials and similar developments had tainted the romanticism of the past, strikes in Britain and the world oil crises of 1973 and 1974 suppressed consumer spending, and growing unemployment and concern for individual welfare began to spark off a new feeling for visual matter. No longer were large-budget publications necessarily the most influential, and the late 1970s saw the birth of a new, austere visual era.

INFLUENCES

1. *Alphonse Mucha, France, c.1900. This mystical art nouveau imagery was paramount in 1960s design thinking. It embodied a love of nature, classic beauty and harmonious lines.*

1

3

2. The Savoy, *Britain, 1896. Drawing by Aubrey Beardsley, an influence on the publications of the youth culture.*

3 & 4. *Fashions, Britain, 1965 and 1970. Fashion followed two distinctive paths: high tech fabrics cut in simple linear shapes and the flamboyant, colourful Indian-influenced style.*

No. 1   Price **2/6** net

January 1896

2

4

5. Self-portrait, *Britain, 1961.*
Peter Blake a foremost
representative of the English pop art
movement. He involved himself in
projects such as the design of the
Sgt. Pepper record cover.

6. *Advertisement, Austria, 1897.
The use of illustration and hand-
drawn type inspired the work of
many pieces of graphic design in
the 1960s and 1970s.*

7. *Guru, India, 1965. Youth
protest sought mystical inspiration
and the guru became a figurehead.
The threat of the nuclear age
brought about the Ban the Bomb
movement and protest singers
such as Bob Dylan, Joan Baez
and Donovan.*

8. *Spaceship, USA, 1969. Man's
technological achievements
culminated with the moon landing.*

9. *Pin Ball machine, USA, c.1950.
These machines decorated in their
totem pole style influenced both
pop musicians and artists alike.*

7

9

NEW DESIGN TRENDS

1. *Edinburgh International Festival, Britain, 1967. Front cover for the Festival programme by Hans Schleger; line illustration and typography reversed out of a tinted portrait image.*

2. *Twen, Germany, 1969. In contrast to the solid black pages, this layout explores the use of compact design within white space. Even the folio has been left off so as not to detract from the effect.*

3. *Oz, Britain, 1967. A parody of other publications, Oz's interpretation of "Playmate of the Month" is an illustrated calendar poking fun at current events.*

The Poster Craze
Die Plakatmanie
La Manie des affiches

12)–15) The
They were s
who thereb
photograph
16)–24) Othe
popular fig
are: 16) Ra
organist in

12)–15) Dies
licht. Der be
men hat, be
graphischer
Plakate hera
16)–24) Weit
kannten Gr
strecken. L
18) Marlon
21) Janis Jo

Photographers/Photographen/Photographes:

12)–15) RICHARD AVEDON
19) 20) 21) BOB SEIDEMANN
22) 23) JERRY BERMAN & ASSOCIATES

Art Director/Directeur artistique:

12)–15) ALLEN HURLBURT

12)–15) La r
Ils ont été e
ainsi qu'on
la photogra
8) 9) Autr
des compos
sont: 16) R
organiste en

…ook first published these portraits of the Beatles. …e by the well-known photographer Richard Avedon, …t psychedelic colour effects can also be obtained by …he portraits were later issued as posters.

…hic posters, ranging from portraits of film stars and …ographic compositions without text. The celebrities …17) W.C.Fields; 18) Marlon Brando; 20) Pig Pen, …l Dead band; 21) Janis Joplin; 24) Twiggy.

…urden erstmals von der Zeitschrift Look veröffent …tograph Richard Avedon, der sie speziell aufgenom …dass «psychedelische» Farbeffekte auch mit photo …icht werden können. Die Porträte wurden später als

…akate, die sich von Porträten von Filmstars und be …photographischen Kompositionen ohne Text er …heiten sind: 16) Raquel Welch; 17) W.C.Fields; …Pig Pen, Organist im Orchester The Grateful Dead; …Mannequin Twiggy.

…fut la première à publier ces portraits des Beatles. …e célèbre photographe Richard Avedon qui prouva …si produire des effets de couleurs psychédéliques par …curement, les portraits ont été édités en posters. …hotographiques, allant des portraits de vedettes à …ographiques «muettes». Les personnages célèbres …; 17) W.C.Fields; 18) Marlon Brando; 20) Pig Pen, …n The Grateful Dead; 21) Janis Joplin; 24) Twiggy.

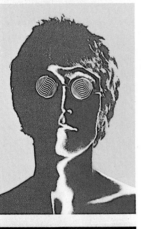

5

6

7

8

9

10

4. Graphis, *Switzerland, 1968. Conceived by Allen Hurlburt, the new concept of photography was produced by Richard Avedon to portray the Beatles.*

5. B. Maclean, USA, c.1968.

6. B. Maclean, USA, c.1968.

7. Wes Wilson, USA, c.1968.

8. Wes Wilson, USA, c.1968.

9. Victor Moscoso, USA, c.1968.

10. Rick Griffin and Victor Moscoso, USA, c.1968. Images 5-10 reflect the influence of psychedelia on layout at this time.

11

11. Graphis, *Switzerland, 1968. This cover was designed in response to the trend of psychedelic imagery.*

1, 2 & 3. Prisunic, France, 1975. A fine example of well-displayed, clear and precise information in a stylish, square format.

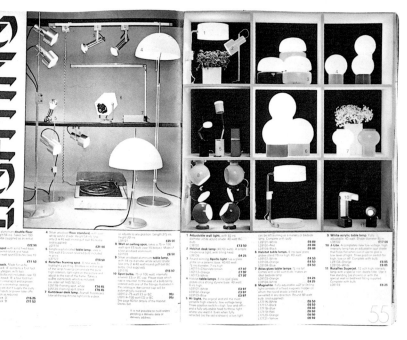

4 & 5. Habitat, Britain, 1971. This revolutionary brochure became a reference point both for a new style of living and for a design approach that influenced the 1970s.

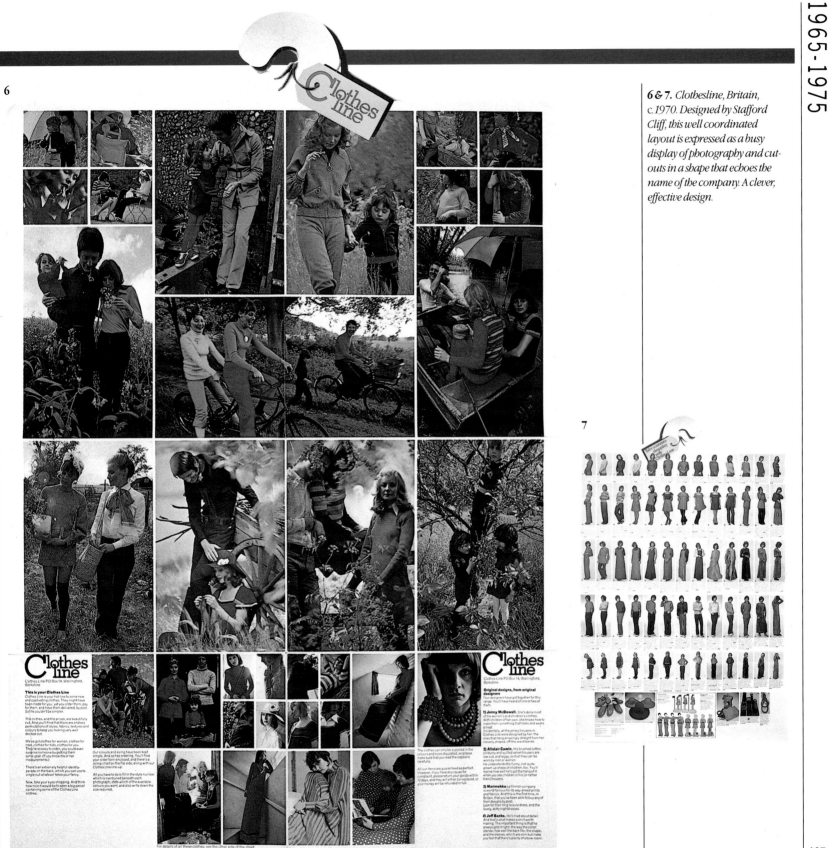

6

7

1

2

POLYPOPS/**GIFT BOXES**

Polypops Gift Boxes Easy to press out
and make up decorative birds and
animals. As a pack for presents and
parcels, or to use as a ditty-box,
snack or tote-box.
Sold in sheet form. Size 18½″ × 22¾″.
P60/1 Bear
P60/2 Lion }   Boxed 10 of each
P60/3 Tiger   design or 50
P60/4 Owl   of one design
P60/5 Puffin
P60/6 Elephant 10 or 50 to a box
P60/7 Jack In A Gift Box,
packed in 10's or 50's

Polypops Products Ltd 216 Tottenham Court Road London W1A 3DH (01) 637 1944/7

3

4

POLYPOPS Childsplay Furniture
is easy to put together.
Simple-to-follow instructions
are enclosed in the flat
Polypops pack.
POLYPOPS Childsplay Furniture
is made up of desks and
tables — and as many chairs
as you want.
POLYPOPS Childsplay Furniture
is for the very young . . .
or for children growing up . . .
or for children playing
grown up.

chair

table

desk

A POLYPOPS Childsplay Desk (or table) makes reading, writing and arithmetic fun to sit down to!

1. Polypops brochure, Britain, c.1975. Hand lettering with distinctive flowery images.
2. Polypops brochure, Britain, c.1975. Simple geometric layout with contrasting weights of type gives a formal setting for the lively and colourful product range.

5

3. Polypops brochure, Britain, c.1975. The current catalogue can be inserted into this outer cover.
4. Polypops brochure, Britain, c.1975. This typical spread divides illustration from text by reversing the copy from a solid background. The products are linked by means of tonal drawings whereas the imaginary settings are left in line.

5. Polypops brochure, Britain, c.1975. Photographs and type are integrated to link the name with the product and create a unity in layout.

MAGAZINES

1. Nova, *Britain, 1973. Art director David Hillman .*

beautiful bodywork

By Pat Baikie
Drawings by Celestino Valenti
Exercise illustrations by Leslie Chapman

This beauty bonus is dedicated to
every woman who normally
goes downhill in winter
and misses looking lovely in spring,
because she's still fighting off
winter – and then summer is upon her
before she knows it and it's too late
to do anything about . . .
dull hair
spotty backs
lazy muscles
give-away wrinkles
flabby arms
bulgy thighs
fat bottoms . . .
and a host of other blemishes.
So we invite you to take a good look
at yourself now and plan positively for
a better-looking summer in '74.
Aim to be healthier, more relaxed and
in good, sleek shape. Your
bodywork schedule develops over
the 6 months from October to
March. It's a progressive plan, starting
with the parts that take
longest to improve and moving on
to the areas which
show quickest results. It's essential
that you complete one month's
routine before rushing on to the next.
Contrary to what you might
expect, the routine doesn't get more as
the months go by; it gets less – so
that by summer '74
you get by with a bare
minimum of beauty maintenance.
The accumulator at the beginning of
each month tells you which
parts of the routine to carry over
and which new areas to concentrate on.
When the 6 months which appear
throughout these pages and pin up the
assemble the pictures which appear
larger-than-life-size lady as a
reminder to keep you up to scratch

DONOVAN'S DOG

STRIKING MATCHES

2, 3 & 4. Nova, *Britain, 1973.*
Distinctively varied layouts use
a combination of grids ranging
from four columns to a single
column.
5. Nova, *Britain, 1973. Nova's*
trademark was the distinctively
designed and progressive covers.

6 & 7. Fortune, *USA, 1967.*
Art directors from the 1930s
included Will Burtin and Leo
Lionni, and from 1963, the art
director was Walter H. Allner.
The typography of this New York
business monthly is plain and
dignified, with commissioned
illustrations and photographs
breaking up the dense
typography.
8 & 9. Playboy, *USA, 1971.*
Art director Arthur Paul.

1, 2 & 3. The Image, *Britain, 1973. Editor and art director, David Litchfield; photographic consultant, David Bailey. This graphic arts and photographic cult magazine features the work of contemporary innovative designers and photographers. It set out to feature and accredit rising stars, and the layout of each page was determined by the style of the work being displayed.*

4

SECRETS OF MALE SEXUALITY

by David R. Reuben, MD

If a woman is searching for sexual satisfaction she desperately needs to know all she possibly can about the innermost sexual secrets of men. Once she is armed with this information, she can face virtually any sexual problem with confidence.

From the book *Any Woman Can!*
© David R. Reuben, MD, 1971
Published by W. H. Allen, £2.50

What are men afraid of sexually? There are six major fears of male sexuality—some conscious, some unconscious:

1 Not being able to have a strong erection.
2 Losing the erection either before intercourse or before ejaculation.
3 Ejaculating too quickly (premature ejaculation).
4 Not being able to have another erection promptly after ejaculation.
5 Not being able to satisfy a woman.
6 Being compared unfavourably with another man when it comes to penis size, potency or sexual skill.

5

VIDAL SASSOON—

How to succeed by really trying

by Deirdre McSharry   photographs by Terry O'Neill

74

6

COSMOPOLITAN

Fourth Issue
June 1972 · 20p

More from the Big New Book Any Woman Can!

Dr Reuben Lets You in On Secrets of Male Sexuality (To Help You Win That Man)

Be the Successful Extra Woman

Yes! There is Life After Divorce—say Tessa Kennedy and Brigid Segrave

Vidal Sassoon Bares His Beautiful Body & Health Secrets

Are You Fed Up With Diets? Then Follow This Great Anti-Diet Inside

Some Psychiatrists Do Have Affairs With Patients

How You Can Be a Sun Goddess This Summer

I Was Never The Princess – Jeannie Sakol's Poignant Novel

4, 5 & 6. Cosmopolitan, *Britain, 1972. An internationally based publication deriving its style from the new-found freedom of the 1960s. It set out to raise the quality and content of women's magazines through its editorial policy and under the art direction of Sue Wade.*

1, 2 & 3. Avant Garde, *USA, 1968. Designed by the leading American typographer and graphic designer, Herb Lubalin, this magazine has an excellent combination of controlled space and type image. Highly praised for its page layouts, it was not noted for its economic success.*

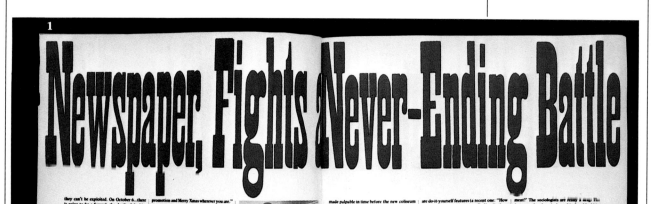

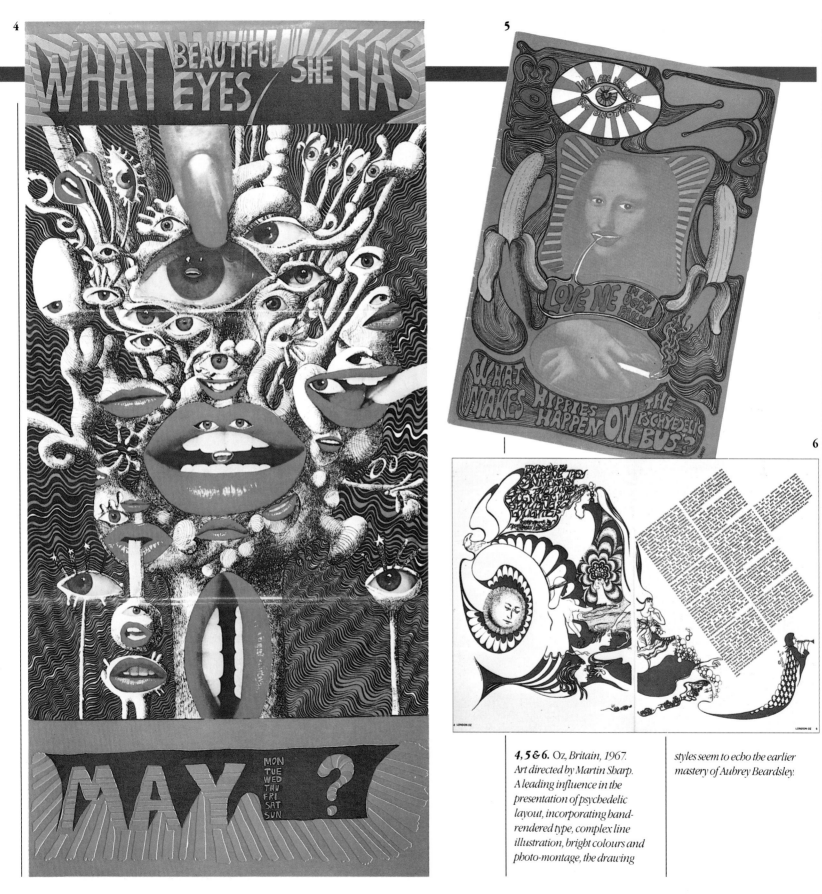

4, 5 & 6. Oz, Britain, 1967. Art directed by Martin Sharp. A leading influence in the presentation of psychedelic layout, incorporating hand-rendered type, complex line illustration, bright colours and photo-montage, the drawing styles seem to echo the earlier mastery of Aubrey Beardsley.

MAGAZINES

2

1

Lyvia Schmetterling träumt

Lyvia Bauer, dunkelbunt wie der Schmetterling, den man Pfauenauge nennt. Haut, die im Schatten eines hellen Olivbraun schimmert. Mandelaugen, die exotischen Sex und heimliche Emanzipation hinter verträumten Kinderblicken zu verstecken wissen. Gestern flirtete der Schmetterling noch haschfrei und beatbunt über „Hair"-Bühnen. Heute zappelt er technicolorig im Zelluloidnetz. Lyvia Bauer, das einzige Mädchen, dem von „Hair" aus der Sprung in die Karriere gelang, spielt ihren ersten Film: „Schmetterlinge weinen nicht". Wie Lyvia Bauer sich in ihrer neuen Welt zurechtfindet, erzählt Anja Hauptmann.

Wie sie abends da so die Hotelhalle durchschwebt, im schwarzen Maxirock und hellgrauer Bluse, die nichts verbirgt, weil nichts darunter verborgen werden muß, drehen sich die Hälse der Herren und auch der Damen wie von ungefähr in die gleiche Richtung. In ihre Richtung. Natürlich.

Wenn es wahr ist, daß zu den wichtigsten Star-Qualitäten dies gehört, daß eine Person einen Raum ausfüllt und beherrscht, sobald sie durch die Tür tritt, dann ist diese Person ein Star. Den Gesichtern der Herren und Damen sehe ich an, daß sie alle meinen, sie müßten ihren Namen kennen. Morgen werden sie ihn kennen.

Und ich vergesse, daß ich schon über eine Stunde auf sie warte.

Sie steht vor meinem Tisch und träufelt ein Grübchenlächeln zu mir herunter, und ich finde, daß sie gar nicht mal eine Ausrede erfinden muß. Sie reicht mir ihre schmale braune Hand mit den entwaffnenden Worten: „Ich hab' verschlafen. Ich war ein bißchen groggy, weil ich heute nachmittag so viel Sekt und Zeugs getrunken hab'. Schlimm?"

Ihr Blick diktiert mir die Antwort. Natürlich nicht schlimm.

Sie setzt sich hin und knackt sich eine frische Osterglocke aus der Blumenvase und steckt sich die gelbe Blüte ins Haar. Mit diesem frechen Lächeln gleicht sie einem thailändischen Knaben, der sich seines Charmes voll bewußt ist, und der mit allem durchkommt, was immer er auch angestellt haben mag.

„Trinken Sie etwas mit mir?" frage ich und sie sagt: „Orangensaft bitte. Alkohol trinke ich nie."

Sie hat also schon vergessen, was sie vorhin über ihre Nachmittagsbeschäftigung sagte. Sie ist der Typ, der immer gleich vergessen darf, was er vorhin erst gesagt hat.

Vergessen auch die Zeit, da ihr die Dorfkinder nachschrien: „Wasch' dich!" Vergessen die Zeit, da sie in der Küche der Bäuerin Eimer voll Kartoffeln schälen mußte. Vergessen, daß der Bauer sie bei Sonnenaufgang mit aufs Feld zur Arbeit trieb. Nicht vergessen: daß irgendwas an dieser Zeit auch schön war: „Das Land. Die Tiere. Die einfachen Menschen. Die Geborgenheit in der verzweifelt engen Bindung zwischen meiner Mutter und mir."

„Ihr Vater?"

„Keine Ahnung. Ich bin ein echtes Nachkriegskind. Mein Vater war ein Farbiger. Mehr weiß ich nicht

Fotos: Josef Hohn

So finden Mädchen einen besseren Chef

3

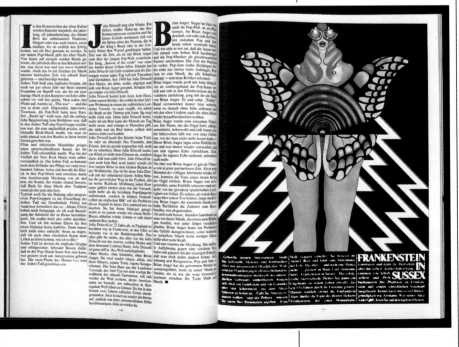

4

2, 3 & 4. Twen, Germany, 1970. Noted for its reversed-out type and use of photography as art subjects, the magazine ran a blue ink beneath the black to improve the blackness and give a richness to the page. Twen used leading illustrators to attract young readers in their twenties (hence the name: Twen).

MAGAZINES

1 & 2. Rolling Stone, *Britain, 1969. One of the first magazines aimed at the TV generation.*

3. Screw, *USA, 1970. A highly controversial underground magazine, art directed by Brill and Waldstein.*

4. IT, *Britain, 1968. Designed to be in tune with the youth of the 1960s.*

5 & 6. Ink, *Britain, 1971. A witty, satirical publication.*

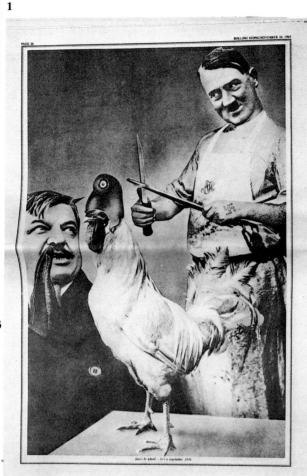

7 & 8. Eye, *USA, 1968. Art director Judith Parker. The masthead lettering style was used as a key element for headings throughout the magazine. The double-page spread demonstrates its unconventionality, even down to the numbering of the personalities*

9 & 10. Time Out, *Britain, 1971. Art director Pearce Marchbank. Devised as a listings magazine for a lively, trendy London audience, it was produced on a tight budget, but included excellent design ideas.*

VACATION BROCHURES

1 & 2. Gaytours, Britain, 1969. Spain's popularity as a destination for package holidays sparked off the mass-production of holiday brochures.

3 & 4. Cunard, Britain, 1966. This brochure retains a traditional, established appearance.

5 & 6. Lunn Poly, Britain, 1966.
Each page attempts to reflect the
characteristics of the holiday
resort.
7 & 8. Skytours, Britain, 1971/
72. By the 1970s the market was
competitive, and brochures had
to be sales orientated.

DIY BOOKS

1. Golden Homes, *Britain, 1973.* An early example of the first do-it-yourself home manuals. Complicated activities had previously been left to experts, but these instruction manual-type publications made it possible for amateurs to carry out complex tasks. This demanded a functional, simple-to-follow layout. Here, photographic images relevant to text are integrated to give the page a friendly and easy-to-follow appearance.

2. Golden Homes, *Britain, 1973.* Another successful innovation is borrowed from the transport signing systems and used to feature individual book sections with specially designed signs.

home engineer 53

Finishes for metal

Most metal objects, whether they are designed to be used indoors or out in the garden, need some form of surface finish, not just for decoration but also to preserve them. For metal used out of doors, the second function is particularly important. But on any metal article, from a kitchen shelf bracket to a garden gate, the finish is important. Using the right finish can enhance the appearance of your home and, as a preservative, it can save you time, trouble and money.

Unprotected metal seldom retains its original brightness for long, even indoors. Except for high-quality 'Sheffield' stainless steel and certain specialized and expensive alloys, all metals gradually discolour in exposure to air. This discoloration takes different forms and happens at different speeds, depending on the type of metal and the environment in which it is placed. For example, a very dry atmosphere will preserve the original bright finish of non-stainless steel for years, whereas the polluted and damp atmosphere of an industrial town will corrode the same type of surface in a few days.

The nature of this discoloration varies with the type of metal—most significantly, whether it is ferrous (iron-based) like steel, or non-ferrous, like aluminium and its alloys, copper

NIGEL MESSETT

and copper-based alloys such as brass. Another important factor is its immediate environment —the materials with which it is in contact, such as wood, other metals, plastics or chemicals. In most cases, it is the oxygen in the air that attacks the surface, any moisture or the airborne acids found in industrial zones accelerating the process. The visible result of all this is corrosion, the commonest—and most damaging—form of which is the rust that affects iron and most ferrous metals.

Iron is, believe it or not, soluble in water, and consequently damp air attacks the surface with great speed to produce *iron oxide*, or rust. Under the right conditions rust spreads quickly and eats the metal right away.

Non-ferrous metals do not rust in the same way. Lead, for example, will corrode in certain conditions, but its corrosion shows as a thin, white powdery coating. A coating of similar appearance, although quite different constituents, appears on aluminium alloys after a while. But these light coatings protect the metal and slow down subsequent corrosion, so that the metal remains strong even if its surface is spoiled.

Corrosion in non-ferrous metals is speeded up by the presence of impurities created by alloying (deliberate mixing with other metals) or as a result of low-grade manufacturing processes that do not refine the metal properly. This is certainly the case with both lead and

aluminium, which have excellent corrosion resistance in their pure state. Another factor that has a great effect on the corrosion resistance of metal is the surface finish. A rough, scratched surface will corrode more quickly than a smooth, polished one.

There are two methods of preventing metal from corroding. One is to cover the metal with a non-porous protective coating such as paint, lacquer or varnish, and the other is to plate the metal with a thin coating of another metal which has a better corrosion resistance than the metal it covers. The second process can be carried out by galvanizing, electro-plating or by an anodic treatment.

Principles of plating

There are several methods of plating. Which one is used depends on the type of host metal (the metal to be plated) and the metal being deposited. For steel and iron, for example, there are two basic treatments: galvanizing and cadmium-plating. Neither process, however, is suitable for the average handyman, since they require elaborate equipment such as heated tanks, powerful and potentially dangerous electrical apparatus and, in the case of cadmium-plating, the use of highly poisonous chemicals.

Galvanizing is normally only used for exterior surfaces, such as corrugated-iron sheeting, gates and fence-posts, because it produces an uneven, mottled surface which is not considered attractive indoors.

An article to be galvanized is first 'pickled' in hydrochloric or sulphuric acid to clean it, after which it is dipped into a bath of molten zinc, which is isolated from the air to stop it from burning up, by means of a layer of flux (which is usually ammonium chloride) floating on the surface. The temperature of the bath is 850 – 900°F (450 – 480°C). Sometimes, particularly when a delicate or intricately shaped article is being galvanized, a small amount of aluminium is added; the effect of this is to make the zinc more fluid, so that thinner coats can be applied

but still ensure total coverage. The thickness of a galvanized coating i 0.0001in. (0.00025mm); the mc spangled surface of the plated article indication of the thickness of the coa larger the spangles, the thinner the coa

An alternative to galvanizing is c *plating*. There is little to choose bet two in the degree of protection they a both are ideally suitable for steel. C plating, however, is more expens galvanizing, and is an electro-plating (see below). After plating, the thin laye mium is slightly porous and, although excellent weather protection and p good key for any subsequent pain porosity means that the bare cadmiu is easily marked by the fingers and h For this reason, articles are usually pu an acid-dip process called *passiva* mediately after plating. This closes t of the metal and makes it much br appearance.

Electro-plating

Electro-plating is a method of co object of one metal with another r submerging both the object and a piec plating metal into a solution that electricity, such as hydrochloric acid

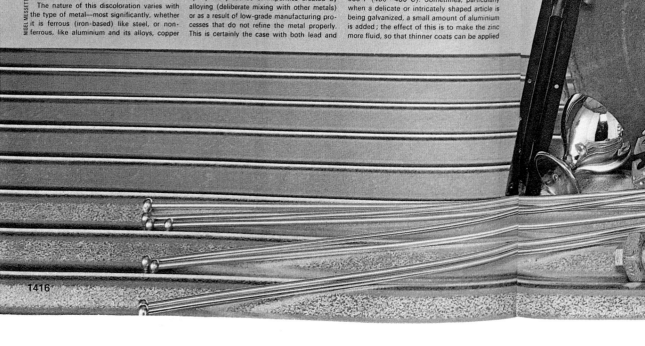

1416

142

and passing an electric current between them. This solution is called the *electrolyte;* it usually contains a *salt* of (or chemical compound containing) the metal to be deposited, and other chemicals to improve the deposit. The metal to be deposited is liberated from the *anode* (the correct name for the piece of that metal) by the electric current and carried across to the *cathode* (the article to be plated), where it settles on and sticks to the surface. Under certain conditions, the anode may be made of an inert metal that does not dissolve; lead anodes are used in chromium plating, and all the chromium comes out of the electrolyte.

As well as the dip process of galvanizing, there is an electro-galvanizing technique, which is preferred in engineering because it gives a more even coating of zinc.

Chromium plating will not stick to bare steel, and the article must be nickel-plated first. To give the best possible adhesion and protection, the process of chromium plating should comprise copper plating, nickel plating and then chromium plating, and the article should be polished between each plating. Very high quality chromium-plating calls for alternate layers of copper and nickel to be applied several times before any chromium is applied at all.

3. Golden Homes, *Britain, 1973.*
4. Golden Homes, *Britain, 1973.*
The signing systems designed for the interior of the book also provide a clever means of unifying the magazine's design.

3

4

CULT BOOKS

1

2

3

It is almost irreverent and certainly irrelevant to think of the Beatles in mundane terms as the pop group who became the biggest rock and roll attraction ever. While their early appearances caused unprecedented scenes of mass hysteria, their music has developed into a fascinating social history of our generation and its culture. It was the realisation of the elevation of pop music and allied pop culture by the Beatles which drew my interest to the possibility of producing this book.

I first became aware of the depth of the lyrics to the Beatles' songs when I went to a party in 1967 during the Sergeant Pepper era. Someone whispered in my ear that Lucy in the Sky with Diamonds was a song about an LSD trip. Although ambiguity in the lyrics to popular music was no new thing, the scale of the various interpretations of the songs on the Sergeant Pepper album so intrigued me that I began reading all the lyrics of Beatles' songs and finding, or imagining, all kinds of hidden meanings. One phrase in particular staggered me: "keeping her face in a jar by the door", from Eleanor Rigby. This seemed to me pure surrealism. And as this was an area in which I was working in illustration I decided in my complete naivety that I should interview the author of the line, Paul McCartney. The result was an article, which when published with my own illustrations, created a deluge of mail. It led me directly to begin planning this book of the Beatles' lyrics.

Altogether something like 180 songs by the Beatles have been published, but since many of the earlier compositions are very repetitive in theme and would not have provided enough different ideas in illustration, we were able to weed them out. Having done that, we sent lists to the 43 contributors and asked them to tick off the ones they wanted to do. Ironically enough it quickly got to the stage where nearly all the ones I wanted to do had been chosen by someone else–but never mind!

What I have tried to do is to present a book which is as entertaining to the eye and the imagination as a Beatles album is to the ear. For an artist it is a challenging exercise to take a lyric and illustrate it. And of course, there is a very long tradition of this. Artists have always illustrated passages from the Bible or from poems, and we have tried to do the same thing here. In a sense...

4

Got to get you into my life

I was alone, I took a ride,
I didn't know what I would find there.
Another road where maybe I
could see another kind of mind there.
Ooh then I suddenly see you,
ooh did I tell you I need you
ev'ry single day of my life?
You didn't run, you didn't lie,
you knew I wanted just to hold you,
and had you gone, you knew in time

we'd meet again for I had told you.
Ooh you were meant to be near me,
ooh and I want you to hear me,
say we'll be together ev'ry day.
Got to get you into my life.
What can I do, what can I be?
When I'm with you I want to stay there.
If I'm true I'll never leave,
and if I do I know the way there.
Ooh then I suddenly see you,
ooh did I tell you I need you,

ev'ry single day
Got to get you in
Got to get you in
I was alone, I too
I didn't know wh
Another road wh
could see another
ooh then I sudde
ooh did I tell you
ev'ry single day
What are you doi

"We were influenced by our Tamla Motown bit on this. You see we're influenced by whateve

?
e.
e.

ld find there.
be I
mind there,
ou.
?
life?

g.''—John

The Beatles Illustrated Lyrics, *volume 1, Britain, 1969. Edited by Alan Aldridge; designed by Gilvrie Misstear and David Hillman.*

1. The single central column of text, supported by airbrush illustrations, occupies the spread and emphasizes the shape and force of colour.

2. Designed emphasis of the layout, with random patchwork sepia photographs. The text is printed on a white panel that echoes the shapes of the photographs.

3. The bold type occupying the page area is complemented by the loose shape made by the airbrush illustration.

4. Pages are linked diagonally by the eyes in the photograph, which creates a negative shape and allows a carefully proportioned space for text.

5. The front cover of The Beatles Illustrated Lyrics, *with layout, design and illustration by Alan Aldridge.*

5

CULT BOOKS

1. Group and Woup, *Britain, 1974.*
Folder/cover by Bob Cobbing. The
letter forms on the cover create
shapes and patterns and so give a
visual dimension to the poetry.
2. Kurrirrurriri, *Britain, 1967.*
Concrete poem by Bob Cobbing.
The layout of this poem has been
created on a typewriter to give
textures and contours.
3. Concerning Concrete Poetry,
Britain, 1976. This cover has been
included to show the influence of
the Futurist Movement on visual
poetry.

4

6

7

5

4. Tree, *Russia, c. 1965. A concrete poem by Valerian Valerianovich Neretchnikov.*
5 & 6. tyger 1 *and* grounrocksa, *Britain, 1971. Two concrete poems by Bob Cobbing.*
7. Zeroglifico, *Italy, c. 1966. By Adriano Spatola. Distorted letter forms create staccato visual patterns.*

1. *Inbucon Limited, Britain, 1968. An almost clinically conceived layout. The type is justified top and bottom, and allowed to express corporate sophistication.*

2. *Inbucon Limited, Britain, 1967. An original and innovative approach. The cover flaps of this square format book unfold to reveal a generous horizontal space and what could almost be a parody of Leonardo's Last Supper.*

3. *IBM, USA, 1975. Hints of Bridget Riley and abstract forms, integrated with structured and formal type, enliven a business-like approach.*

4. *IBM, USA, 1965. A page dedicated to a computer range presents technology in visual form, and the range number decorates the white space with well chosen type forms.*

1

Inbucon Limited. Annual Report & Accounts for the year ended 31 March 1968

Inbucon

2

3

IBM

Annual Report 1975

4

36o

The widespread acceptance of System/360 made major demands throughout IBM in 1965. New laboratory and plant facilities were being built, advanced concepts in production, programming, and servicing being developed, and a worldwide education program begun. On the following pages, you will see several of the events which shaped this intensive Company-wide effort.

Right: Intricate electronic circuit patterns, drawn with the aid of a computer, are among hundreds which make up System/360's complex circuitry. Shown here on a glass master negative, reassembled approximately five times, the patterns are transferred, developed and etched onto printed circuit cards in a highly automated process.

6

nbucon Limited, Annual Report & Accounts for the year ended 31 March 1967

NEWSPAPERS

1. The New York Times, *USA, 1969.*
2. Evening Standard, *Britain, 1966.*
3. Tampa Tribune, *USA, 1968. Each newspaper carries its own identity in its style, with a carefully chosen number of typefaces for display headings.*

4. The New York Times, *USA, 1969. This unique inside layout shows the newspaper's use of graphic design to create a layout that is both memorable and important enough to reflect this major achievement.*

5 & 6. Suburban Press, *Britain, 1972. In contrast to the established press, the mood of the young generation and their attitude to the modern urban environment is expressed through this publication. Designed by Jamie Reid.*

7. Evening News, *Britain, 1973. The headline acts almost as an advertisement for the content of this newspaper.*

8. Le Monde, *France, 1970. The restraint with which the French publication presents the dramatic news borders on timidity.*

9. The Times, *Britain, 1966. The first occasion on which news and photographs appeared on the front page.*

THEATER

1, 2, 3, 4 & 5. *Edinburgh International Festival, Britain, 1967/1970/1972. Designed by Hans Schleger. A selection of innovative layouts showing a variety of techniques in the use of photographic images from montage, line, tints and combined cut-out images. The layouts also use a variety of reversed-out and overlapping colour techniques.*

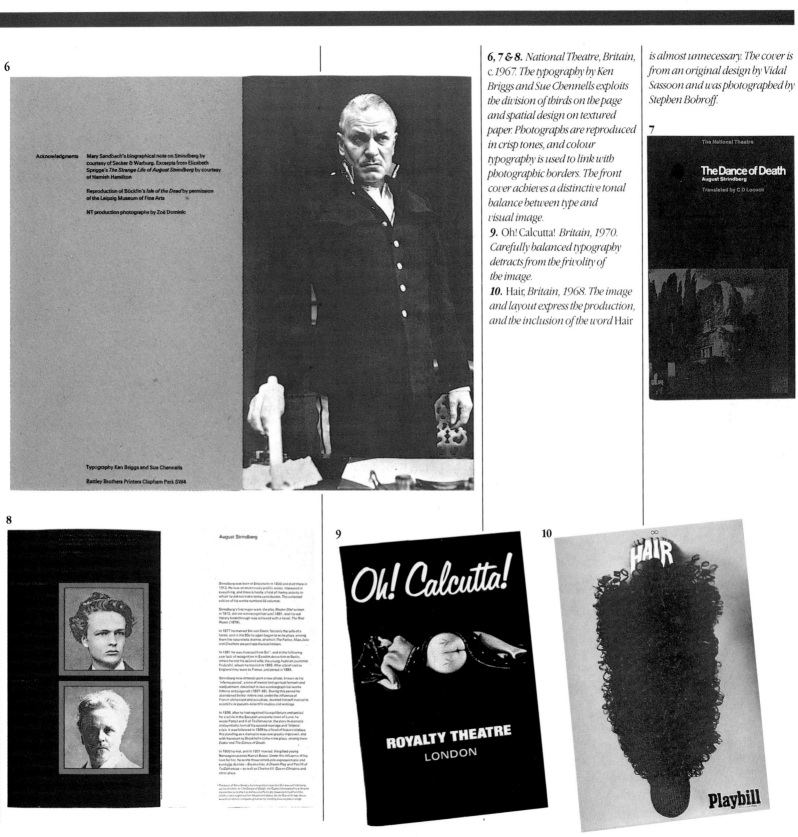

6

Acknowledgments
Mary Sandbach's biographical note on Strindberg by courtesy of Secker & Warburg. Excerpts from Elizabeth Sprigge's *The Strange Life of August Strindberg* by courtesy of Hamish Hamilton

Reproduction of Böcklin's *Isle of the Dead* by permission of the Leipzig Museum of Fine Arts

NT production photographs by Zoë Dominic

Typography Ken Briggs and Sue Chennells

Battley Brothers Printers Clapham Park SW4

6, 7 & 8. *National Theatre, Britain, c. 1967. The typography by Ken Briggs and Sue Chennells exploits the division of thirds on the page and spatial design on textured paper. Photographs are reproduced in crisp tones, and colour typography is used to link with photographic borders. The front cover achieves a distinctive tonal balance between type and visual image.*

9. *Oh! Calcutta! Britain, 1970. Carefully balanced typography detracts from the frivolity of the image.*

10. *Hair, Britain, 1968. The image and layout express the production, and the inclusion of the word* Hair

is almost unnecessary. The cover is from an original design by Vidal Sassoon and was photographed by Stephen Bobroff.

7

The National Theatre

The Dance of Death
August Strindberg

Translated by C D Locock

8

August Strindberg

9

Oh! Calcutta!

ROYALTY THEATRE
LONDON

10

HAIR

Playbill

Typeface broadsheet, Britain, 1988. Designed for Esselte Letraset Ltd by David Quay.

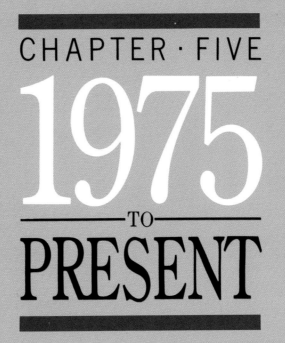

CHAPTER · FIVE

1975

TO

PRESENT

INTRODUCTION

Design in the mid-1970s was undergoing a reappraisal. The relative stability of the economy and growth in design businesses had led to the clients becoming the dominating factors in the development of graphic design ideas. Commercial control of visual matter was conditioned by company policy. The designer's task was to sell the client's product strictly according to marketing strategy, and the marketing departments of publishers, magazines, advertising agencies and other commercial concerns, relying as they did on the structured feedback of market research departments, became the dominant commercial force.

Design had become part of the establishment business sector, and consultancies such as Michael Peters and Wolff Olins were now firmly locked into corporate presentation in the promotion of sales. Products underwent microscopic scrutiny, and the tiniest detail was considered for its sales/design effectiveness.

British art schools, now moving more towards the commercial realities of the design industry, were offering structured courses that prepared students for the activities of the commercial world. Students had always had access to the past through their studies; now they worked with a specific view to future employment. Their studies of art and design history provided a foundation on which they could base their future visual careers.

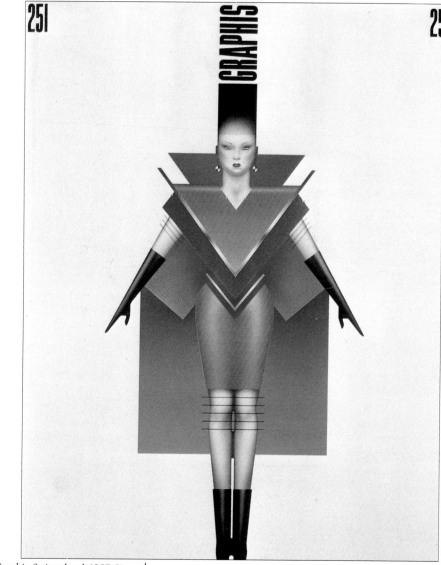

Graphis, *Switzerland, 1987. Since its inception in 1944, Graphis has become an international reference for the advances in graphic design. This image reflects the work of Alan Jones the pop artist, the best of punk and futuristic style.*

God Save the Queen, *Britain, 1977. The effect of punk art was to loosen up the whole idea of what was possible in graphics. Jamie Reid's bold statements opened up uncharted graphic territory.*

The Influence of Punk

However, the creative energies of 1970s youth were not directed solely towards the established and conventional sectors. Under the surface, new waves of cultural rebellion were reacting against the mainstream. A radical reaction, with the anti-establishment music of punk groups and their associated design ideas, set the tone for a regeneration in creative image-making. When the Sex Pistols launched their record, "God Save the Queen", the designs for its publicity, created by Jamie Reid, provoked genuinely impassioned responses.

As the middle classes enjoyed more and better

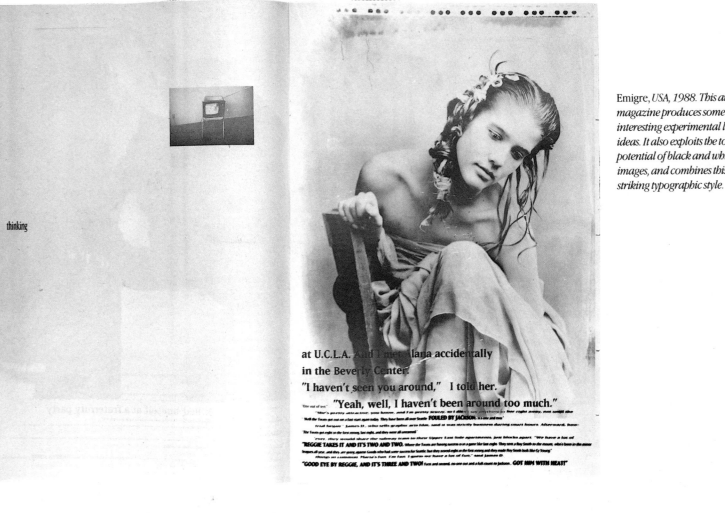

thinking

at U.C.L.A. And I met Lana accidentally
in the Beverly Center.
"I haven't seen you around," I told her.
"Yeah, well, I haven't been around too much."

Emigre, *USA, 1988. This arty
magazine produces some
interesting experimental layout
ideas. It also exploits the tonal
potential of black and white
images, and combines this with
striking typographic style.*

designed information, and a broader choice of reading matter, other, less well-off people saw the imagery in a different light. As their access to the expensive new technology was limited, they devised ways in which designs could be put together and reproduced using basic and readily available materials. Old sheets of Letraset, with few remaining characters, were placed together to create words in type. Photocopies of cheap photographs gave a linear quality that gave scope for experiments; the cutting of newsprint and a sympathy with old typesetting processes were passionately exploited. The revulsion against the sophistication of style that was seen in this period was expressed in a desire for individuality.

In parallel with this revolution of ideas on the fringes of mainstream design, technology itself was creating a new awareness of the potential of design layout. It was becoming easier to produce experimental images with the aid of computer-assisted and colour-efficient copying equipment. *I-D* magazine was quick to incorporate the styling used in the "random" design methods of punk art, using expressive page layouts to explore street fashion through distorted and regenerated photographic images. As a commercial enterprise, *I-D*, which was set up by Terry Jones, its art director and co-publisher, became influential among aspiring young designers.

INTRODUCTION

More Dark than Shark, *Britain,
1986. Assorted images design
group, headed by Malcolm Garrett
and Kasper de Graaf, set out to
explore the art potential of
graphic projects.*

More Dark than Shark, *Britain,
1986. The front cover for this
publication, with its apparent
three-dimensional surface, is
overlaid by type that is linked
through an irregular grid.*

At the same time Neville Brody, art director of *The Face* magazine, was exploiting the technological revolution by exploring the potential of computer-modified type in the production of new imagery and page layouts. His work, which referred back to the historical sources of design, had unique characteristics that could have been generated only by the new technology available to Brody.

The new imagery was not confined to Britain. In Italy, stylish magazines with a satirical photographic content were communicating new wave imagery, and publications like *Moda* were leading this trend. In America, *Emigré*, an arty cult magazine, was also exploring new layout ideas through the application of the new technology.

Mainstream designers, with their international reputations, were engaged in the restructuring and presentation of new and restyled publications. Alan Fletcher's design for *24 Ore*, an Italian financial newspaper, employed a nine-column grid, which was flexible enough for both horizontal and vertical design layouts. Willy Fleckhaus had set the tone for this with *Twen* in the early 1960s, with a grid formation that gave unlimited scope for column widths and picture cropping. Indeed, grids give an underlying sense of design with highly sophisticated controls on modern layout, and the increasing development and understanding of grid design led to consistency in publication image. *Elle*, for example,

Letraset se enorgullece de presentar una familia de tipos totalmente nueva, diseñada por David Quay. Arta es un estilo muy actual sin serif, derivado de las formas de letras tradicionales. Quay afirma que se inspiró en la naturaleza condensada de la Blado Italic de la monotipia. Su formato poco habitual -la cursiva sólo difiero do loc caracteres normales en la caja baja-contribuye a dar a Arta el grado de individualidad que necesita el especificador tipográfico moderno.

Arta Light

Arta Book

Arta Book Italic

Gama, Esselte Letraset Ltd, Spain, 1987. Typeface designed by David Quay. Innovative layout by Quay and Gray.

with its roots firmly in France, could be transported lock, stock and barrel into a number of international versions through the consistent base of a common grid design policy.

Design Today

The 1980s have identified the designer as the cultural innovator of our times. Designers and design houses are now sought for their particular creative style, which is controlled and governed by senior members of the house or group, whose vision imposes consistency in their innovative work. Many design groups offer their own style and approach to solving design problems, and they set out to show the client how to appreciate their visual and cultural leadership. This, of course, represents something of a reversal from previous years, when the client tended to control the creative parameters within which the designer could work.

In the past few years there have been radical changes, even in the design of newspapers. New publications are now expected to offer precision in layout and styling that meets the high expectations of their readers, and modern technology allows full colour to be designed into the pages.

Graphic design has become a competitive art form within itself. The quest for new and innovative approaches to design has always been, and continues to be, led by those artists and designers who are prepared to reach beyond the current trends and fashions. In the last century designers from all nations contributed to advances in graphic design techniques and the elements that play an essential part in the creative process, but the emphasis has shifted away from the ideas and struggles inherent in a changing society in which the artist's role takes account of industry and technology. Crucial to this change has been the influence of innovative designers in Holland. From van Doesburg's early design concepts to the work of Dutch designers such as Studio Dumbar and Total Design, the climate of experimentation has encouraged exciting work, which uses the early formulae, which were revolutionary in their own time, as a means of discovering exceptional solutions to the creation of exciting layout design.

No designer in the 1930s could have known how influential the French publication *Mise en Page* would be. Today the Dutch experimental book *Vorm in de Maak* parallels Tolmer's work and could well exert an influence over layout ideas for some years to come.

INFLUENCES

1. *Cover, Germany, 1920. Kurt Schwitters, influenced by Kandinsky and the Dadaists, extensively experimented in collage, and had a passion for using household rubbish.*

2. *Cover, Germany, 1919. Georg Grosz's powerful satirical drawings, and their rebellious stance, have been the inspiration for many new illustrative forms.*

3. *God Save the Queen, Britain, 1977. Jamie Reid was the first punk artist to exploit the powerful potential of the found image. His work links to the satirical artists of the past.*

4. *Club chair, Bauhaus, 1925. Designed by Marcel Breuer for Kandinsky. Its perfect geometric balance and exploitation of materials and space continue to exert an influence on all areas of design sixty years after its manufacture.*

5

8

6

8. For the Voice, *USSR, 1923. El Lissitzky's simplification of visual layout continues to be the inspiration for much of today's design. His genius in exploiting artistic form from simple elements relates closely to the architectural concept behind the Pompidou Centre.*

9

5. *Pompidou Centre, France, 1977. The Pompidou Centre, designed by Rogers, Piano and Franchini, marks a revolution, in its honest, unadorned use of materials, of a design which shows the construction's functional elements on its surface.*

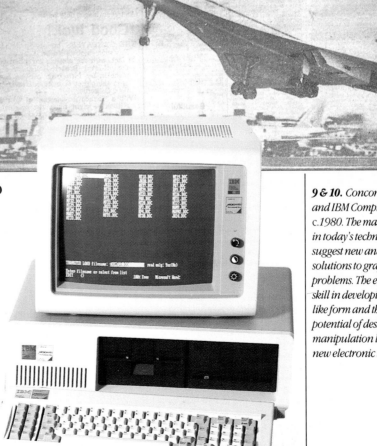

7

6 & 7. Typographica, *Britain, c.1950. Typographic experimentation in the 1950s, and the work of Herbert Spencer, continue to be an inspiration.*

10

9 & 10. *Concorde, Britain, 1976 and IBM Computer, Britain, c.1980. The massive developments in today's technology continue to suggest new and original creative solutions to graphic design problems. The engineering and skill in developing this sleek bird-like form and the immense potential of desktop computer manipulation lead the way into a new electronic visual age.*

MAGAZINES

1 & 2. Crafts, *Britain, 1986-7. An innovative approach for this type of magazine, using the techniques exploited by the early punk designers.*

3 & 4. City Limits, *Britain, 1982. This London magazine broke away from* Time Out *in 1981*

Compagne di vita **3** *La donna orientale*

L'EROTAOISMO DELLA GEISHA

QUESTO MESE

WOODY ALLEN

5, 6 & 7. King Manifesto, *Italy, 1988. This statement of style, firmly rooted in the tradition of Marinetti and Futurism, is a direct descendant of the large format* King Moda.

THE WEIRDEST THING IS
WE'LL DO IT FOR FREE!
VIDAL SASSOON

Il cinema? È altrove...

Hollywood? Non abita più qui

E' una città degradata in cui si muove un'umanità povera e marginale. Una città di fantasmi; attori, registi, comparse: scomparsi. Ma sul set di «KingModa» sono tornati i *Grandi Personaggi*: la Starlette, la Piscina, il Produttore, la Coppia Divina…

i-D
FUN'N
DUST
SUN'N
LUST
LOVE AND ROMANCE

8 & 9. i-D, *Britain, c. 1981. Following the format created by Terry Jones, the magazine continues to generate aggressive and confident new images for a progressively fashionable audience.*
10 & 11. King Moda, *Italy, 1987. The forerunner of King Manifesto makes exciting use in its layouts of apparent accidents, cleverly using them to communicate a new layout style.*

MAGAZINES

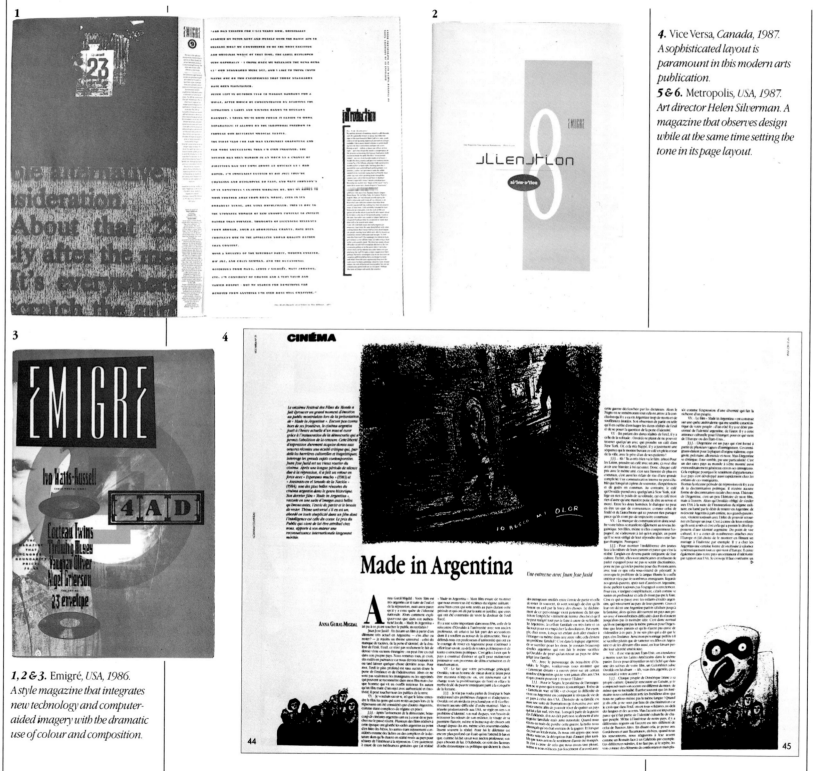

1, 2 & 3. Emigré, *USA, 1986.*
A style magazine that integrates new technology and computer-aided imagery with the dramatic use of colour and composition.

4. Vice Versa, *Canada, 1987.*
A sophisticated layout is paramount in this modern arts publication.

5 & 6. Metropolis, *USA, 1987.*
Art director Helen Silverman. A magazine that observes design while at the same time setting the tone in its page layout.

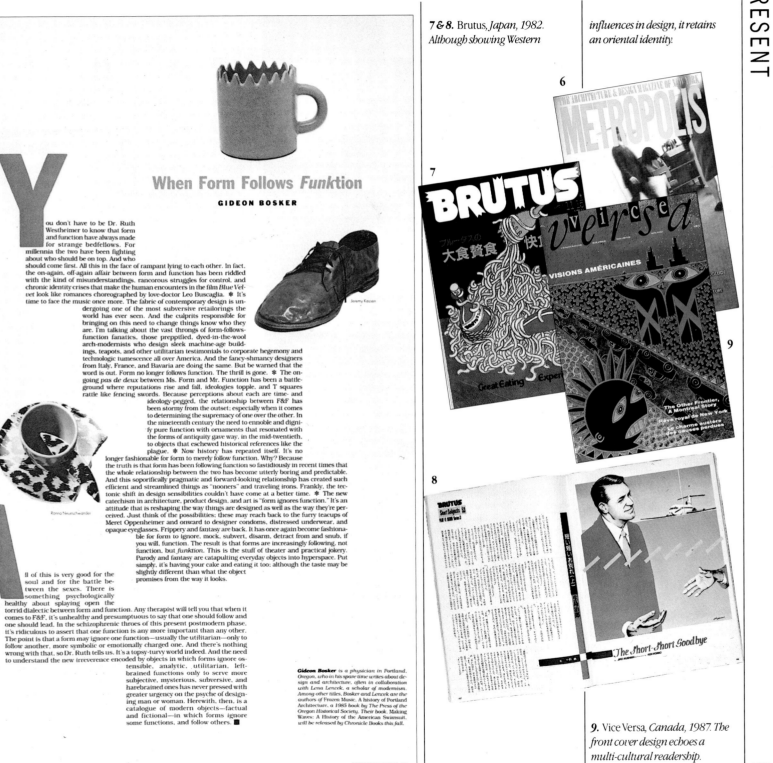

METROPOLIS MAY 87 53

7 & 8. Brutus, *Japan, 1982.* Although showing Western influences in design, it retains an oriental identity.

9. Vice Versa, *Canada, 1987.* The front cover design echoes a multi-cultural readership.

MAGAZINES

1. Avantgarde, *Britain/France/USA, 1980. The large-format, stylish arts and fashion magazine, with Martin Hooper as art director.*
2, 3 & 4. Avantgarde, *Britain/France/USA, 1983. Following in the footsteps of Fleckhaus, this magazine makes extensive use of black pages and "arty" photography.*

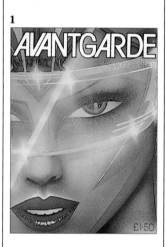

1

AVANTGARDE
£1·50

3

ROARING, SPHINXLIKE, AND GENTLE
Ricki Amy talks to Helen Mirren, currently starring in the two Royal Shakespeare Company productions.

2

HAUTE COUTURE HAIR

SCHUMI

avantgarde hair

4

AVANTGARDE
PARIS   MILAN   LONDON   NEW YORK

french & italian
COLLECTIONS

5, 6, 7 & 8. Paris Match, *France, 1989. This publication combines stylish typographic pages with integrated type and photography, making ordinary photographs and page layouts appear quite special.*

ILLUSTRATION & TEXT

1. *Anita Kunz, USA, c.1983. The illustration is carefully used to frame the subjects, and this is echoed in the typographic layout with its white border or frame.*

2. *Simpson Paper Co., USA, 1988. Milton Glaser's high standard of design and illustration still sets today's visual pace. The central illustrated letter form links the illustration with the page of text.*

3. *Fernando Botero, USA, 1983 The illustration on this page complements the illustrative use of type, which appears to form the shape of a skull on the right-hand side of the page.*

4. *Milton Glaser, USA, 1983. A founder of the Push Pin Studios, Glaser (b.1930) is an illustrator and designer with an international reputation whose work can be found adorning the pages of leading publications.*

1

2

3

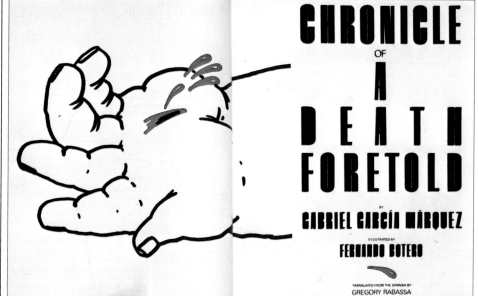

VANITY FAIR

MARCH 1983

$3.00

4

6

5

'Wash your mouth out with water,' my mother would scold whenever I used a swear word as a child. The instruction to scrub oneself was in its own way a revealing one, reflecting the assumption that to articulate certain words in certain settings was actually dirty and contaminated not merely the person who uttered them but everyone else in earshot. Within such a model of social relations, swearing was on a par with relieving or exposing oneself in public. It was quite simply an affront to good manners and, if it involved the use of a religious word or image, an outrage to the Deity. It involved, in effect, the breaking of a taboo.

At the present time, however, the sounds of the taboo breaking are deafening: muffled oaths, ripe curses, obscene rantings, profane swears – on stadium terraces, tennis courts, motorways, around dinner tables, at business meetings, even in the House of Commons. Prominent individuals from John McEnroe to Bob Geldof are noted for their verbal laxity, while only the shortsighted can avoid lip-reading the mouthed profanities of sportsmen frustrated by the goal disallowed or the cricket appeal turned down.

The arena of sport is the one in which the swearing explosion is most audible. In cricket we have had an England captain and a Pakistani umpire exchange the kind of language one might expect from dock-workers. But the curses rain down everywhere else as well. On stage, Caryl Churchill's biting satire on yuppies in the City, *Serious Money*, scarcely raised an eyebrow, yet its language would have made a 1950's navvie blush. In film, the sight of John Gielgud mellifluously articulating expletives in the movie *Arthur*

would have seemed as likely a decade previously as seeing Noel Coward picking his nose.

The readiest explanation for this turn of events owes something to the argument that swearing is all about the release of pent-up and unbearable tension. The actual physical explosion involved in cursing – and many of the more popular maledictions do involve guttural ejaculations of a forceful kind – serves to defuse tension and ease strain. Ours is a time when tension is alleged to be high. We work to tight deadlines in pressurised settings. We commute to and from work in degrading, travelling conditions. We are subject to arbitrary delays, have to cope with the vagaries of machinery, and have to endure other people caught in the same ghastly mess. It is a commonplace observation that people swear under pressure, but commonplace or not, the view holds the key to why swearing is like smoking for many – it is a regrettable activity but without it the swearer, like the smoker, feels he would burst.

I once worked for a surgeon who outside the operating theatre was a bachelor of the most amiable temperament – gentle, relaxed, quiet-spoken and shy to the point of immobility. You would readily entrust your grandmother or your cat to him, and many of his friends regularly did both. Once inside the theatre, though, he was a man transformed. At the slightest set-back, such as a nurse somewhat slow to pass an instrument or an anaesthetist inclining to garrulousness, he would explode demonically, hurling instruments like a demented football hooligan and cursing like the proverbial trooper. The nuns, for it was a religious

hospital, purported to be shocked and indeed most probably were, but they had learned to act as if this was the most normal way to behave, as if every surgeon they had ever encountered used their operating facilities to regress to infancy and bawl and shout like a frustrated toddler. Only when the operation was completed and the gloves and mask removed, would he return to the sweet, charming anonymity of his non-professional self.

But swearing is unlikely merely to be about tension relief, and the increase in swearing cannot be attributed entirely to the fact that we live in difficult times. Swearing is also inherently violent. It constitutes a verbal assault from which people can be seen to recoil as if literally struck. Interestingly enough, the growth of physical violence in contemporary society appears to be accompanied by a comparable growth in the willingness of people to pummel their opponents with verbal insults. The curse is used to goad, to humiliate, to frustrate. The existence of shocking words, and images conjured up by them, means that an impact can be made, a sense of shock and outrage provoked, without the protagonist having to turn to physical violence to make his point. Yet, paradoxically, when these words no longer achieve their purpose, the provocateur can only give up or resort to actual, bodily assault. When words lose their power to offend, we lose an important means of communicating offence, a means that does not involve physical outrage and does not, in the majority of cases, leave irreversible scars.

If I am right and swearing has a crucial link with violence, then one might hypothesise that men, the

❋ ❋ ❋ !

Rude, lewd and appallingly crude, today's language is enough to make a sailor blush. Anthony Clare curses our four-letter world

102   ILLUSTRATIONS: IAN POLLOCK

Brian Grimwood
through an open window

5. Ian Pollock, Britain, c.1985. The distinctive, mocking style echoes the work of Georg Grosz with a polemic force. The construction of illustration and text cunningly interlocks using overspill matter from the illustration.

6 & 7. Brian Grimwood, Britain, c.1975 and 1987. The centrally positioned, ragged form of the musician is echoed on the facing page by the centrally positioned ragged type. Grimwood's style has changed over the last decade as can be seen by comparing the musician with the earlier work.

TYPOGRAPHY

1. Hand-drawn type by Neville Brody, Britain, 1983. This style of type is based on brushmarks.

2 & 3. Typeface by Neville Brody, Britain, 1986. Used initially for Arena magazine and later developed into a lower case

alphabet, this face is reminiscent of the elegant style of Bodoni.

4. Jamie Reid, Britain, 1977. Breaking with graphic traditions, Reid's revolutionary approach to type and image set the punk style for at least a decade.

5. Jamie Reid, Britain, 1976. This example reveals Reid's three-dimensional approach to type as an image.

1

2

3

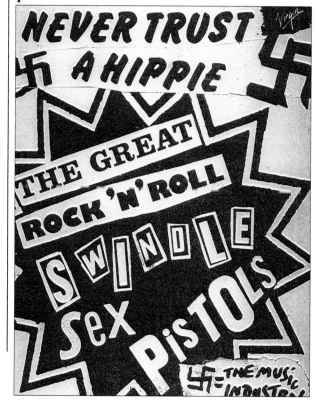

4

5

6

EIGHT FACES FROM THE '50s

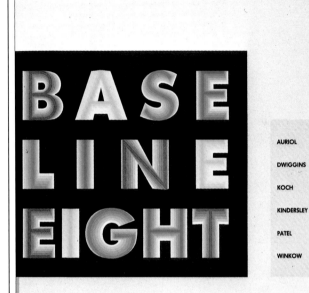

7

INCLUDING.....

BASE LINE EIGHT

AURIOL

DWIGGINS

KOCH

KINDERSLEY

PATEL

WINKOW

INTERNATIONAL

TYPOGRAPHICS

MAGAZINE

8

6. *Esselte Letraset Ltd, Britain, 1988. Distinctive typefaces are given a dynamic look by being presented in a modern layout.*

7. Baseline Eight, *Britain, 1988. The technological advances and the history of typefaces are presented in this magazine. The front cover shows just how far modern typography can be manipulated: the typography has been produced on an Ikarus computer using Futura light, book, medium, semi-bold, bold and extra bold.*

8. U&Lc, *USA, 1988. The inspiration and force behind this publication was Herb Lubalin, whose work in developing modern typography is probably unparalleled. This publication, which is issued by the International Typeface Corporation, provides a platform for the most inspired application of type, both past and present.*

BROCHURES & CATALOGS

1. Préférences d'Habitat, France, 1987-8. A modern concept of page layout in which the outer area is as important as the page layout itself.

2. Mappin & Webb, Britain, 1987-8. A similar format to the French Habitat brochure (above), but the layout is restrained by retaining the central blocks for the pictures and text.

3. Habitat, Britain, 1989.
4 & 5. Habitat, France, 1987-8. The cover reflects a high-tech range of products using styles borrowed from the past, and the spread opens up to present a vertical format in which type and photography are laid out to give a busy high-tech appeal.

CITIZEN

JAMES J. MURPHY
Professor of Physics
Chairman, Physics Department, Iona University
New Rochelle, New York

James Murphy has taught physics for twenty-seven years at a small college in New Rochelle. Nonsectarian, Catholic in tradition, and administered by the Congregation of Christian Brothers, Iona is a place Professor Murphy finds comfortable and peaceful.

Professor Murphy's preface to a student manual for one of his department courses tells much about him.

"In our culture, the progress of science and technology holds primary responsibility for the accelerating rate of societal change.... Like the Industrial Revolution, the current computer, nuclear, and genetic technologies will bring about a global transformation which is nearly impossible to overestimate. To exercise our options as individuals and our responsibilities as participants in a democracy, we will have to converse with scientists and comprehend their methods and reasoning. Scientific and technological literacy are quickly becoming valuable assets in most occupations and are essential aids to good citizenship.

"Can the education you are acquiring today place you at any advantage in the future world? Iona College believes not only that it can, but that it should and must ..."

James Murphy received his Ph.D. at Fordham. His research work has included the study of the problem of radon in the indoor atmosphere, and the effects of pulsed nuclear resonance in magnetically-ordered binary alloys of transition metals.

REFORMER

MARY ELEANOR CLARK
Professor of Biology
San Diego State University

My serious teaching didn't really begin until I saw the smog in Southern California. I'd been in England for seven years. I was horrified. People seemed to pay no attention to the mess they were creating. When I found I was being asked to teach 250 students in introductory biology I thought, this is my opportunity.

"I began teaching environmental issues and health issues in relation to basic biology. I incorporated concerns about alcoholism into the cell structure and function lecture. I incorporated ideas about pollution into the environmental lectures. I talked about air pollution in terms of photosynthesis. I simply employed problems that had biological implications.

"I began to realize that the biological aspects of our problems are connected with economics, political science, our values, our history, our religious outlook. In my experience, when subjects are taught so that they throw light on contemporary questions and issues, students are immediately interested.

"I hope my students take away with them an attitude that it is important to be aware of the world and how it works—not merely because it will make their lives more interesting but also because it is a duty for all of us to participate in creating a better world."

Mary Eleanor Clark majored in Biochemistry at Berkeley and there received her doctorate in Zoology. She has taught, lectured, and conducted research in France, England, and Sweden. At San Diego State since 1969, she teaches biology, physiology, and endocrinology. She also teaches interdisciplinary courses that cover global issues and ethical dilemmas as they relate to the use of resources.

A

ART

"I like to show people that there are shortcuts ..."

PAUL RAND

CONTENTS

6. *Simpson Paper Company, USA, 1988. A promotional catalogue, designed and illustrated under the direction of Milton Glaser, that makes use of the paper qualities.*

7. *Next Directory Preview, Britain, 1989. This visual theme is used in the layout of all the Next publications of this period.*

8. *Laura Ashley Home Catalogue, Britain, 1989.*

9. *Murata Godo Inc., Japan, 1982. Spacious and minimal in its approach to layout.*

カラーコーディネーション

INFORMATION DESIGN

LIVING AT THE ISLAND CLUB

In any society, any environment, any group of people, there are always the discerning few whose aspirations are higher than others . . . a select band of individuals who will be satisfied only with the very best. For them, work is a preoccupation: recreation and leisure an essential enrichment.

It is for these people that the Apartments at the Island Club have been created.

Burrell's Wharf is, in itself, symbolic of an enhanced lifestyle. A unique location, where the character of a Victorian Wharf has been both preserved and blended with a broad range of amenities, providing an integrated environment of the highest possible standards.

Standing at the centre of Burrell's Wharf is the Island Club. Once known as The Platehouse, it was here that the steel plates for Brunel's maritime masterpiece, the Great Eastern, were formed. Now, the building forms the centrepiece of the Burrell's Wharf development, containing London's most exclusive, recreational, leisure and fitness facility, together with 23 apartments of character and luxury, in a rare combination.

The character of the apartments is itself a unique feature incorporating restored details of the original building; massive roof trusses, arched warehouse windows, and mellow brickwork, together create an atmosphere of timeless solidity.

All apartments have their own distinction: The exclusive Penthouse in the tower, with its arched and porthole windows provides commanding views of the central courtyard and river on three sides. High in the eaves of the building, loft studios feature 16ft high ceilings, galleried kitchens and terraces. Whilst the one and two bedroom apartments offer full width windows, balconies and their own individual views. Naturally all apartments are generously carpeted, and comprehensively equipped to make a living environment that is as luxurious and as comfortable as possible.

The deciding factor in choosing an apartment at the Island Club must, however, be its proximity to the club itself. The combination of such appealing living accommodation with an unparalleled range of recreational facilities in a single building provides you with a unique quality of life.

Created within a building which is a fine example of Victorian architecture, Isambard Kingdom Brunel constructed the world's first iron steamship, the 'Great Eastern', here — the Island Club is now the focus of another great idea.

More than simply a number of luxury facilities available under one roof, the Island Club focuses on meeting the social, recreational and fitness needs of the entire Burrell's Wharf community.

Your Health and Fitness — A Way of Life

1 & 2. Kentish Homes Limited, Britain, 1989. A large format information brochure for a new style of life in London's Docklands. Illustrative matter at the head of the page with apparently random photographs are overlaid with an impressive drawing printed on tracing paper to divide the spread.

ISLAND APARTMENTS LEISURE COMPLEX

Where the quality of life is enriched by the quality of leisure

3. Pleasure Bold Shaded, Britain, 1988. The richness of colour and energetic expression in layout make this information sheet, designed by David Quay, a useful reference point.

4. AIGA, USA, 1989. A narrow
horizontal format which makes a
feature of the black, spiral binding.
Confident, offset illustrations are
complemented by the formal type.
5. Kentish Homes Limited, Britain,
1989. Large luxury format
exploiting grainy black and white
photography, busy illustrations
and a central band of copy.

6. Lynwood, Britain, 1988.
Designed by Conran Design
Group.
7. Exhibition invitation, Britain,
1988. Designed by Pat Schleger for
an exhibition of Zero's (Hans
Schleger) work.

1 & 2. Total Design, Holland, 1985. Designed by Frans Lieshout for the 20th anniversary and exhibition of the Total Design Group, this is a revolutionary design.

3. 20th-Century Architecture, Britain, c.1985. Written by Lance Knobel, published by Faber & Faber.

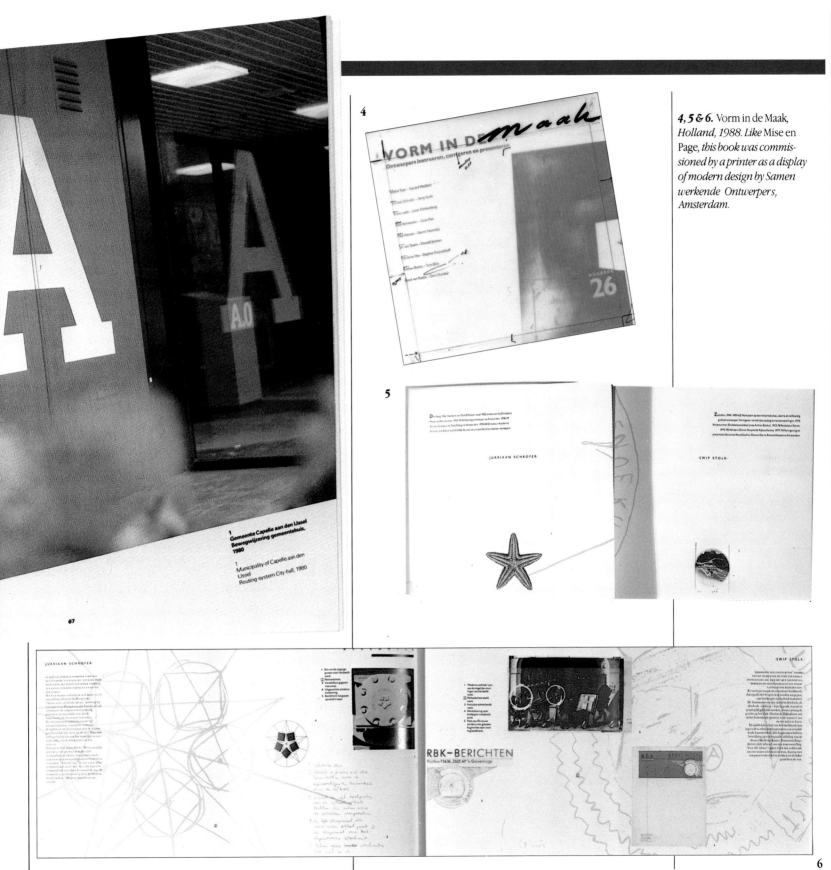

1
Gemeente Capelle aan den Ussel
Bewegwijzering gemeentehuis,
1980

1
Municipality of Capelle aan den
Ussel
Routing-system City-hall, 1980

67

4, 5 & 6. Vorm in de Maak, *Holland, 1988. Like* Mise en Page, *this book was commissioned by a printer as a display of modern design by Samen werkende Ontwerpers, Amsterdam.*

SOPHISTICATION & STYLE BOOKS

1 & 2. More Dark Than Shark, *Britain, 1986. Designed by Assorted Images under the direction of Malcolm Garrett.*
3 & 4. The Roux Brothers on Patisserie, *Britain, 1986. A high-class book on French patisserie.*

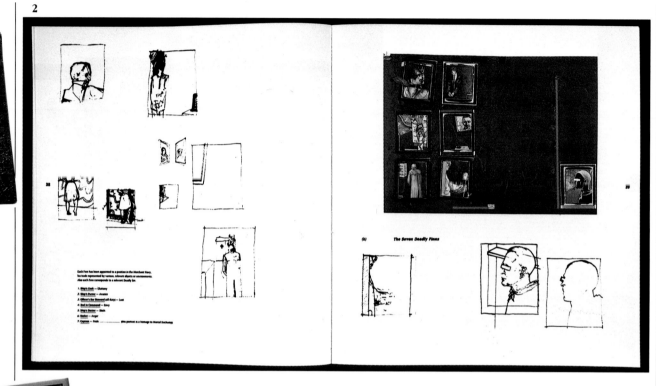

5

PRESS ADS, USA

1/2/4 *CLIENT:* LINCOLN MOTOR CARS

3 *CLIENT:* OLDSMOBILE

5 *CLIENT:* CHRYSLER

6 *CLIENT:* BUICK

6

5. Creative Director's Sourcebook, *Britain, 1988. Published by Macdonald Orbis and designed by Quarto Publishing. The ultimate in sophistication.*

6. The Human Body, *Britain, 1983. An educational pop-up book for adults, combining excellent engineering, design and layout.*

7. Creative Director's Sourcebook, *Britain, 1988. A bold but sophisticated layout of type on this title page.*

7

SOPHISTICATION & STYLE BOOKS

1, 2 & 3. Penguin, Britain, 1989. A new concept in book covers and layout design. In true Penguin tradition, new territory is explored.

4.

PICADOR

THE TIN DRUM
by GÜNTER GRASS

It was the publication of *The Tin Drum* in 1959 that launched Günter Grass as
an author of international repute. Bitter and impassioned, it delivers a scathing
dissection of the years from 1925 to 1955 through the eyes of Oskar
Matzerath, the dwarf whose manic beating on the toy of his retarded
childhood fantastically counterpoints the accumulating horrors of Germans
and Poland under the Nazis.

'Funny, macabre, disgusting, blasphemous, pathetic, horrifying, emetic,
erotic, it is an endless delirium, an outrageous phantasmagoria in which dust
from Goethe, Hans Andersen, Swift, Rabelais, Joyce, Aristophanes and
Rochester dances on the point of a needle in the flame of a candle that was not
worth the game'
DAILY TELEGRAPH

'The novel is as monstrous as its hero, pullulating with a kind of anti-life for
which one of the most horribly memorable images of the book, a horse's head
seething with live eels, serves as a suitable emblem. Günter Grass may have
written the nearest thing to a literary masterpiece his generation is capable
of producing'
DAVID LODGE, THE SPECTATOR

'This is a big book in every sense, full of extraordinary scenes and characters,
even on a single reading it seems prodigally rich in comic invention, and
demands to be worried at again and again'
JULIAN MITCHELL, THE SUNDAY TIMES

THE TIN DRUM · Günter Grass

GÜNTER
GRASS

THE TIN
DRUM

PICADOR

ISBN 0-330-30554-9
90000
9 780330 305549

6.

PICADOR

CAT AND MOUSE
by GÜNTER GRASS

Cat and Mouse was first published in 1961, two years after Günter Grass's
controversial and applauded masterpiece, *The Tin Drum*. Once again Grass
turns his attention on Danzig in a subtle blend of humour and power that
ostensibly relates the rise of the oversized Joachim Mahlke from clown to hero.
But Mahlke's outlandish antics hide the darkness at the heart of a country torn
by Nazi violence, the war and its aftermath.

Critical acclaim for Günter Grass

'Grass is one of the master fabulists of our age'
MICHAEL RATCLIFFE, THE TIMES

'Grass is a playful, exuberant writer'
PAUL BAILEY, EVENING STANDARD

'Grass is probably the nearest thing we have to a certain genius
in living novelists'
MARGHANITA LASKI

CAT AND MOUSE · Günter Grass

GÜNTER
GRASS

CAT AND
MOUSE

PICADOR

ISBN 0-330-30556-5
90000
9 780330 305563

5.

PICADOR

DOG YEARS
by GÜNTER GRASS

First published in 1963, *Dog Years* is perhaps the most violent and unrelenting
of Grass's novels. In a fusion of mythology and reality, magic and romance,
it charts forty years of German history commencing from 1917, with
the objective of exposing the madness of a society that bred and nurtured
the horrors of the Third Reich then anaesthetised itself with the chaos
of disintegration.

'Günter Grass releases, against the grain of history, a troop of obsessional
characters, armed often with magical or at least disconcerting powers, who
gnaw through the madness of the Third Reich and the chaos of the collapse,
into the complacent fabric of modern West Germany'
NEAL ASCHERSON, NEW STATESMAN

'Forty years of twentieth-century German history observed through a massive
fable about men and dogs. Mad, Gothic, repetitive and bitterly funny'
MICHAEL RATCLIFFE, THE SUNDAY TIMES

DOG YEARS · Günter Grass

GÜNTER
GRASS

DOG
YEARS

PICADOR

ISBN 0-330-30555-7
90000
9 780330 305556

*4, 5 & 6. Picador, Britain,
1989. The choice of type, linked
to a sensitive understanding of
space, makes the typographic
layout of these covers
outstanding and noteworthy.
This series of books has been
given a distinctive identity by the
carefully chosen range of
coordinated colours.*

NEWSPAPERS

1. Today, *Britain, 1986. The first issue of the first colour daily tabloid newspaper in the United Kingdom. This four column, plus one, front page format sets out to divide the major news stories in a bold slab serif typeface with reversed-out cross heads in sans serif. Colour is used liberally but to great effect.*
2. Today, *Britain, 1986. A six column inner page format, with sans serif headings. The body text produces a light greyness to help elevate the colour pictures off the page.*

1

TODAY

A lifeline for Kirsty
SEE CENTRE PAGES

TUESDAY MARCH 4, 1986 · 18 PENCE
IN BRIEF

US mole was Prime's KGB successor

SECOND SPY INSIDE GCHQ

EXCLUSIVE by PAUL MARKILLIE

SAVAGED: David

Inquest on dog victim

AN ESCAPED Boxer dog called Digger is believed to have savaged seven-year-old David Clarke to death.
An inquest will now be held on David, found dead near his home in Hoton, Leicestershire. 6

Teachers settle

A PROVISIONAL settlement of the year-long teachers' dispute was reached last night. The deal involved pay rises of between 6.9 and 8.5 per cent in return for talks about teachers' appraisal as part of a longer-term settlement. But the NUT refused to lift its ban on voluntary duties, so some disruption is likely.

Ice heroine

A TEENAGER owes his life to an attractive 21-year-old after she kept him warm by sharing his sleeping bag.
Robert Cuesta, 17, of Clarke's Road, Bournemouth, was with Sally and two other boys on a Duke of Edinburgh Award climbing exercise in the Peak District when he collapsed as the temperature dropped to -8C. Sally, a trainee veterinary nurse, put Robert in his sleeping bag and climbed in on top.

...st Jameson

...rek Jameson launches ...h twice-weekly column ...h comments on Tony ...ncock and the police.
Page 19

...atan trial

THE Bishop of Chichester, the Very Rev. Eric Kemp, ...l, has told Maidstone Crown Court how he became suspicious of Derry Mainwaring Knight. Knight is accused of conning rich churchgoers out of £200,000. 3

AN AMERICAN suspected of having replaced KGB master spy Geoffrey Prime in British Intelligence is being investigated by MI5.
The spy catchers are tracing the activities of computer expert Ronald Pelton. Like Prime, he worked at the top-secret Government Communications Headquarters in Cheltenham.
MI5 has been ordered to establish whether Pelton, 44, of the US National Security Agency — GCHQ's sister organisation — was the mysterious second KGB agent who took over from Prime after his cover was blown.
The latest revelation about the controversial spy centre will seriously embarrass both the US and British governments. Following the Prime affair, Mrs Thatcher — under strong American pressure — ordered closer scrutiny of GCHQ staff.

Awaiting trial

A Government inquiry by the Security Commission warned that another KGB mole might have been selling secrets to the Soviets undetected.
The commission's report said: "Our inquiry has been unable to eliminate the possibility that Prime may not have been the only source of information available to the Russians regarding the signals intelligence operations of the NSA and GCHQ."
Pelton is now under arrest in the United States. He was seized by the FBI last November after a month-long surveillance operation, and is awaiting trial on espionage charges in Baltimore, Maryland.
Since his arrest, American security officials have been quizzing GCHQ staff who worked with him when he was at GCHQ during the Seventies.
After he left the spy base, Pelton returned to the NSA in America. But he left under a financial cloud in May 1979. Eight months later, according to an alleged confession to the FBI, he offered his services to the KGB.
When Prime was jailed for 35 years at the Old Bailey in November 1982, Pelton began earning thousands of dollars from Soviet paymasters

RONALD PELTON: under arrest

based — as in the case of Prime — in Vienna.
After his arrest, Pelton described to FBI officers a shadowy existence which had striking similarities with that of 48-year-old Prime.
Both were trained as Russian linguists. Both worked on highly sensitive satellite intelligence systems. And both visited Vienna, where they were controlled by the same KGB officer.
Security services have investigated the possibility that Prime acted as a recruiter for the KGB. One of his main tasks may have been to identify potentially weak members of staff at GCHQ who might bow to offers of Soviet money or blandishments.
It is possible that Prime may even have pointed out Pelton to his Soviet bosses as a possible spy in the making.
FBI chiefs, aware that the KGB only pays for top-grade intelligence, have concentrated on finding out what secrets Pelton had to offer. There are three main theories.
● He knew of a special NSA

Turn to Page 2

Our Royal Today

THIS historic colour picture of The Queen in Sydney this morning marks the first issue of TODAY. It was transmitted in seconds down a telephone line on a Scitex scanner, the first

2am Colour Exclusive

time computer technology has been used to transmit news pictures from Australia to Britain.

ALARM: Bishop

OPINION 15 ● TV 24 & 25 ● ENTERTAINMENT 26 ● LETTERS 29 ● WEATHER 33 ● SPORT 38-44

2

"It beats hanging around street corners"

A lifeline for Kirsty and Adam

THE DIVINE FELLOWSHIP – WORKING WITH YOUTH

3. The Independent, *Britain, 1986.* The masthead for this new heavyweight newspaper has a traditional feel achieved by the fine serifs and linear shadow. A distinctly transatlantic look. The eight-column grid format also has many sound precedents.

4. The Independent, *Britain, 1986.* The solid newsy spread is broken up by the introduction of a five-column grid placed within a six-column grid space. This lifts the main article giving it more prominence.

NEWSPAPERS

1. The Guardian, *Britain, 1989. The redesign of this newspaper generated much controversy over newspaper layout.*

2.

2. The Guardian, *Britain, 1989. In the redesign the way information was presented was also rethought. This resulted in the newspaper being divided into pullout sections appearing on different days.*

3.

3. The Guardian, *Britain, 1973. By making a comparison with* The Guardian *as it previously appeared, it is clear just how radical these design changes are.*

HUGO YOUNG ON THATCHER, PART V — PAGE 25

Westland: how ambition, intrigue and duplicity came close to wrecking her and forced out Leon Brittan

Books, page 29

Penelope Lively: the drama of suffocated lives

Review, page 27

Tony Benn calls for an end to blasphemy

30p
Friday
April 7
1989
Published in London
and Manchester

The Guardian

Thatcher tells Gorbachev: We want you to succeed ● US ripples summit harmony with disclosure of Soviet arms to Libya

PM hails 'peaceful revolution'

Hella Pick, Jonathan Steele and John Carvel

MRS Thatcher last night portrayed the London summit as a success, and praised President Gorbachev's "peaceful revolution", despite British protests over Soviet bomber sales to Libya and Mr Gorbachev's irritation with the United States for revealing the deal at this time.

If it's Thursday, then it must be Thatcherland

Eyewitness

Andrew Rawnsley

Libya leak 'came from Bush team'

Martin Walker in Washington

The rest of the news

Labour split on intervention

Namibian hope

WHICH OF THESE LANGUAGES WOULD YOU LIKE TO SPEAK?

Tick the one you want to speak in 3 months time...

4

THE BIG NEWS PAPER

DAILY EXPRESS

Wednesday, January 29 1986 20p ★ TV Pages 12 and 13 THE VOICE OF BRITAIN

Fireball

Last moments of doomed shuttle

Horror blast...smoke and flames fill the sky yesterday as an explosion rips space shuttle Challenger apart, killing seven

FULL, DRAMATIC STORY AND PICTURES: PAGES 2, 3, 5 and CENTRE PAGES

5

⊞ **Rocky Mountain News**

DENVER, COLORADO
★ Tuesday, January 28, 1986 **EXTRA** 25¢

SHUTTLE EXPLODES

All 7 in Challenger crew die after liftoff

The fireball that signaled disaster for shuttle mission 51-L occurred only 1 minute, 15 seconds after liftoff from Kennedy Space Center. NASA officials said there were no apparent problems at the time.   *ASSOCIATED PRESS*

4 & 5. Daily Express, *Britain, 1986.* Rocky Mountain News, *USA, 1986. Newspaper layout is international as these two examples show. The addition of colour makes a difference to the impact of the American layout.*

7. The Observer, *Britain, 1989. This fashionably designed supplement for a Sunday newspaper is a platform for modern photography. The typography tonally complements the black and white image.*

8. The Observer, *Britain, 1989. Echoing the format and layout of the early De Stijl.*

9. The Observer, *Britain, 1989. The photograph has been printed as a duotone of green and black with white-out text, but the layout is hinged on the subtle use of red.*

6

Sunday Telegraph

7 DAYS

6. Sunday Telegraph, *Britain, 1989. This larger than usual newspaper supplement is halfway between a newspaper and a magazine .*

7

INTERVIEW

John Sessions didn't go to Cambridge, he can't remember famous quotes and says he is continually bruising his shins on the inanimate world. So how did the 'little smart-alec with the big nose' manage to get his own television series? LYNNE TRUSS talks to the unpretentious improvisationist

Impressions of Sessions

PHOTOGRAPHS BY JOHN STODDART

'ACTUALLY, I'M NOT VERY GOOD AT ENJOYING MYSELF'

8

MAGAZINE **OBSERVER**

THIRTY YEARS OF CASTRO'S

NEW SERIES: THE HEAD GARDENERS NEW COLUMN: SIMON HOGGART

SECTION 5

WHY DYLAN? THE HOT DOG SQUAD TROUSER PRESS

JOHN SESSIONS Lasting Impressions

9

1. Cool Tempo, *Britain, 1986. Record sleeve design by Neville Brody using computer modified type giving a distinctly Suprematist feel.*

1

2 & 3. *Hanover Acceptances Group, Britain, 1988. This corporate publication uses images manipulated through desktop publishing methods, where image and tonal qualities are made to harmonize with typographic elements.*

2

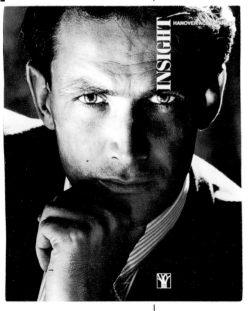

3

December 1988

insight

hanover news

4. Code, *Britain, 1987. This symbol, created on computer by Cornel Windlin and Neville Brody for a record by Cabaret Voltaire, breaks down to read the word 'code' and was used in a large format as a layout in the record sleeve.*

4

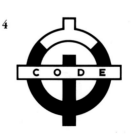

5. Kurtis Blow, Party Time, *Britain, 1985. In this experimental record cover design the diagonal steps of type are held in place by the circular pattern formed by the title.*

5

ARTIST TIME

KURTIS
BLOW

★ THE GO·GO EDIT

6

Paris

COMING TO BE KNOWN
AS THE *FAST YEARS*: A SOCIAL EXPERIMENT
TO STEER A COUNTRY INTO THE FUTURE....

7

FREDERIC ANDREI WAS THE OPERA-
LOVING POSTBOY IN JEAN-JACQUES
BENEIX'S MOVIE *DIVA*, THE FRENCH FILM
THAT HELPED DEFINE THE STYLE OF POP
VIDEOS AND MOVIES IN THE EIGHTIES.
HE'S JUST COMPLETED *PARIS
MINUIT*, WHICH
HE DIRECTED
AND STARS IN.

6 & 7. The Face, *Britain, 1986.*
Designed by Neville Brody.

8

true west!

8. The Face, *Britain, 1985. Strong
shapes build strong layouts, and
Neville Brody successfully
generated some excellent versions.*

9 & 10. Cabaret Voltaire, *Britain,
1984. The ultimate control comes
from computer-generated imagery.*

9

cabaret
voltaire

MICRO-PHONIES

10

CABARET
VOLTAIRE

INDEX

CREDITS

Quarto would like to thank the following for their help with this publication and for permissions to reproduce copyright material.

pp10/11: (1) By courtesy of the Board of Trustees of the Victoria and Albert Museum;

pp12/13: (1) By courtesy of the Board of Trustees of the Victoria and Albert Museum, (2) (3) Pat Schleger;

pp14/15: (1) By courtesy of the Board of Trustees of the Victoria and Albert Museum, (2) The John Frost Historical Newspaper Service, (3) Mappin and Webb, (4) Backnumbers;

pp16/17: (1) (3) (4) By courtesy of the Board of Trustees of the Victoria and Albert Museum, (2) (5) Pat Schleger;

pp18/19: (1) (4) By courtesy of the Board of Trustees of the Victoria and Albert Museum;

pp20/21: (1-6) Pat Schleger;

pp22/23: (1) (5) (6) (8) (9) Pat Schleger, (2) (3) (4) (7) By courtesy of the Board of Trustees of the Victoria and Albert Museum;

pp24/25: (1-10) Backnumbers;

pp26/27: (1-4) By courtesy of the Board of Trustees of the Victoria and Albert Museum;

pp28/29: (1) St. Brides Printing Library, (2) Hammersmith Library, (3) Alan Swann, (4) By courtesy of the Board of Trustees of the Victoria and Albert Museum;

pp30/31: (1-4) St. Brides Printing Library;

pp32/33: (1-7) By courtesy of the Board of Trustees of the Victoria and Albert Museum;

pp34/35: (1) (4) Pat Schleger, (2) (3) By courtesy of the Board of Trustees of the Victoria and Albert Museum;

pp36/37: (1-7) The John Frost Historical Newspaper Service;

pp38/39: (1-5) By courtesy of the Board of Trustees of the Victoria and Albert Museum;

pp40/41: (1-3) By courtesy of the Board of Trustees of the Victoria and Albert Museum;

pp42/43: (1) (2) Savoy Theatre, (6) (7) Savoy Hotel, (3-5) Retrograph Photographic Archive;

pp44/45: (1) (4-7) Savoy Hotel, (2-3) Kevin Chappell, Gilbert and Sullivan Collection;

pp46/47: (1) By courtesy of the Board of Trustees of the Victoria and Albert Museum';

pp48/49: (1) David King, (2) (3) Pat Schleger;

pp50/51: (1) Penguin Books, (2) Alan Swann, (3) Pat Schleger;

pp52/53: (1) David King, (2) (8) (9) Pat Schleger, (3) (6) By courtesy of the Board of Trustees of the Victoria and Albert Museum, (4) The Tate Gallery;

pp54/55: (1-2) Pat Schleger, (3-10) Backnumbers;

pp56/57: (1) By courtesy of the Board of Trustees of the Victoria and Albert Museum, (2) Backnumbers, (3) Pat Schleger, (4-9) Alan Swann;

pp58/59: (1-7) Pat Schleger, (8-10) Alan Swann;

pp60/61: (1) By courtesy of the Board of Trustees of the Victoria and Albert Museum, (2-3) Paul Diner, (4) Alan Swann, (5-8) Penguin Books;

pp62/63: (1-7) Alan Swann;

pp64/65: (1) By courtesy of the Board of Trustees of the Victoria and Albert Museum, (3) Dover Publications Inc;

pp66/67: (1-7) Backnumbers;

pp68/69: (1-6) Backnumbers;

pp70/71: (1-4) Backnumbers, (5-6) © The Walt Disney Company;

pp72/73: (1-4) (6) (7) Backnumbers, (5) (8) (9) Pat Schleger;

pp74/75: (1) (4) By courtesy of the Board of Trustees of the Victoria and Albert Museum, (2) (3) (5-7) Retrograph Photographic Archive, (8-9) Savoy Hotel;

pp76/77: (1-3) Pat Schleger, (4) Reproduced with the permission of HMSO, Crown Copyright, (5-6) Backnumbers;

pp78/79: (1-6) The John Frost Historical Newspaper Service;

pp80/81: (1) Alan Swann;

pp82/83: (2) Graham Pilgrim Automobile Historian, (3) Pat Schleger;

pp84/85: (1-2) Penguin Books, (3) Thomas Cook;

pp90/91: (1-2) Backnumbers, (3-4) Sunday Times Magazine;

pp94/95: (1-9) The John Frost Historical Newspaper Service;

pp96/97: (1) The Vintage Magazine Company, (2) (6) Stafford Cliff, (3) Life Magazine, (4) Sunday Times Magazine, (5) McCalls, (7) The Beatles Monthly Book;

pp98/99: (1-4) Alan Swann;

pp100/101: (1-6) Milton Glaser;

pp102/103: (1-6) Milton Glaser;

pp104/105: (1-7) Pat Schleger;

pp106/107: (1-3) Alan Swann, (4-7) Raymond Mander and Joe Mitchenson Theatre Collection;

pp108/109: (1-6) Pat Schleger, (7-8) Alan Swann;

pp110/111: (1-5) Graham Pilgrim Automobile Historian;

pp112/113: (1-3) Cunard, (4) Pat Schleger, (5-6) Retrograph Photographic Archive;

pp114/115: (1-2) Pat Schleger, (3-4) (7) Thomsons, (5-6) Thomas Cook;

pp116/117: (1) Stafford Cliff;

pp118/119: (1) Graham Pilgrim Automobile Historian;

pp120/121: (1) EMI Records, (2) Twen;

pp122/123: (1) (9) Alan Swann, (3) By courtesy of the Board of Trustees of the Victoria and Albert Museum, (4) Daily Telegraph Colour Library, (6) Pat Schleger, (7) Sheridan Photo Libray, (8) NASA USA;

pp124/125: (1) (4) (5-11) Pat Schleger, (2) (3) Stafford Cliff;

pp126/127: (1-3) (6-7) Stafford Cliff, (4-5) Habitat;

pp128/129: (1-5) Edward Pond;

pp130/131: (1-4) (8-9) The Vintage Magazine Company, (6-7) Pat Schleger;

pp132/133: (1-5) Alan Swann, (6) Cosmopolitan;

pp134/135: (1-6) Stafford Cliff;

pp136/137: (1-4) Stafford Cliff;

pp138/139: (1-2) (4-6) Bob Cotton, (3) (7-10) Stafford Cliff;

pp140/141: (1-8) Thomsons;

pp142/143: (1-4) Marshall Cavendish;

pp146/147: (1-3) (5-7) Bob Cobbing/Peter Mayer, (4) Jean-Francis Bory;

pp148/149: (1-2) Pentagram, (3-4) IBM (USA);

pp150/151: (1-4) (7-9) The John Frost Historical Newspaper Service, (5-6) Jamie Reid;

pp152/153: (1-5) Pat Schleger, (6-8) The National Theatre, (9-10) Raymond Mander and Joe Mitchenson Theatre Collection;

pp154/155: (1) Reproduced by kind permission of Esselte Letraset;

pp156/157: (1) Jamie Reid, (2) Pat Schleger, (3) Emigre;

pp158/159: (1-2) Malcolm Garratt, (3) Reproduced by kind permission of Esselte Letraset;

pp160/161: (3) Jamie Reid, (6-7) Pat Schleger, (8) David King, (10) QED;

pp162/163: (1-2) Crafts, (3-4) City Limits, (5-7) King Manifesto, (8-9) i-D, (10-11) King Moda;

pp164/165: (1-3) Emigre, (5-9) Stafford Cliff;

pp166/167: (1-4) Avantgarde, (5-8) Paris Match;

pp168/169: (1) Anita Kunz, Playboy, (2) Milton Glaser, (3) (4) Vanity Fair, (5) Gentlemen's Quarterly/Ian Pollock, (6) ABSA/Brian Grimwood, (7) Brian Grimwood;

pp170/171: (1-3) Neville Brody, (4-5) Jamie Reid, (6-7) Reproduced by kind permission of Esselte Letraset;

pp172/173: (1-5) (9) Conran, (6) Milton Glaser, (7) Next PLC;

pp174/175: (1) (2) (5) Kentish Property, (4) Vanderbyl design, (7) Pat Schleger;

pp176/177: (1-2) Total Design, (3) Faber & Faber, (4-6) Samenwerkende Ontwerpers;

pp178/179: (1-2) Malcolm Garrett, (3-5) (7) Quarto Publishing, (6) Jonathan Cape;

pp180-181: (1-3) Penguin Books, (4-6) Picador;

pp182/183: (1-4) The John Frost Historical Newspaper Service;

pp184/185: (1-5) The John Frost Historical Newspaper Service;

pp186/187: (1) (4-10) Neville Brody, (2-3) A.J. Vines

Every effort has been made to trace and acknowledge all copyright holders. Quarto would like to apologize if any omissions have been made.